T0243255

BERBER&Q
ON VEGETABLES

BERBER&Q
ON VEGETABLES

JOSH
KATZ

RAW & RIPPED

GRILLED & CHARRED

SEARED & SAUTEED

SLOW-COOKED & BRAISED

POACHED & STEAMED

CONDIMENTS & LARDER

ROASTED & SMOKED
WOOD-FIRED & BAKE
STUFFED & SKEWER
8 PUREED & CHOP
FRIED & BATTERED

can rise to their occasion and make the most breathtaking of dishes. They
them a kaleidoscope of colour, while varying in texture and carrying such
nges of flavour that, contrary to popular belief, they have never required mea
olster. It is just about knowing how to cook with them. Here is a collection of
at shows you how to do just that – presenting roots, greens and legumes in a
stripping away those outdated connotations often associated with vegetarian
ffering a fresh approach to everyday cooking.

I'm a huge advocate of the Mediterranean way of eating, where vegetables
share centre-stage with meat and fish. Anyone who has dined at my
restaurants, Berber & Q and Shawarma Bar, will be familiar with our cauliflower
shawarma. It has been our signature dish since we first opened in 2015, and I
think what people love about it is that it challenges archaic ideas of what a
vegetarian dish might look and taste like. It's a whole cauliflower, glistening and
charred, doused in buttery spices and dripping with tahini, pomegranate and
rose petals. It delivers on every level.

Cauliflower shawarma may be the most iconic of our non-meat dishes, but
Berber & Q has always been about putting vegetables on an equal footing
with meat and fish. We work with what is available seasonally (for this is when
vegetables will taste their best) and challenge ourselves to think about the
cooking methods, sauces and seasonings that will bring the most out of each
piece of produce. We're very proud to have created dishes like Chilli-roasted
Pumpkin (page 38) which appears on our menus every autumn, or our
ever-present Grilled Broccoli (page 56) which, for me, has been a life-changing
way to cook this simple green.

Although I have cooked in restaurant kitchens for many years, I am at heart a
home cook. A charcoal grill or a barbecue is certainly not essential for cooking
the recipes in this book. I developed all of these recipes in a domestic kitchen
In fact, I start this book with a chapter on raw vegetables because first I think
we can all benefit from learning to appreciate the unadorned sweetness of a
summer tomato, the peppery crunch of a radish or a tangle of shredded
greens that are tossed together to make a slaw. Elsewhere in the book I grill,
roast, pickle and purée, all with the same intention – to bring the most out of
the vegetables.

I started writing this book in 2020 when, in the midst of unpredictable

northern Ibiza. It was a welcome chance to slow down and ended up being a poignant time for me. I feel that the past few years have forced us to re-evaluate what is really important, how we relate to each other, to our world and to our food. I am not proposing – or dismissing – vegetarianism as a way of life, but I do believe in working towards more balance with our diets and that we can all make individual, small adjustments that can have a significant impact on the environment for future generations. There is much evidence to say that reducing our collective consumption of meat and fish in favour of a more plant-based diet will be to the benefit of our planet.

I hope this cookbook not only results in a new-found appreciation of cooking vegetables but is also a small step towards making a positive lifestyle change. By capturing the honest beauty of smoky aubergine, a velvety beetroot or the nutty sweetness of a caramelized artichoke, I hope to empower home cooks with all the tools to make bold, bright and flavour-packed dishes. The time has come to embrace vegetables with open arms.

HOW TO **USE THIS BOOK**

I have come to realize that there are three types of home cook: those who follow recipes to the letter, those who use recipes as inspiration and freestyle it, and those who are somewhere in between, substituting this and that according to personal taste and what is in their cupboards. Whatever type of cook you are, I hope this book opens the floodgates for new ways to cook with vegetables.

If you are keen to make swaps and changes, then I wholeheartedly encourage you and offer some tips in this section on how to do just that. If you choose to be exact in following the recipes, I am confident they will serve you well. However, do be mindful that there are many variables to affect the outcome of a recipe: ingredients can vary, ovens can operate at slightly different temperatures, pots and pans can conduct heat differently depending on their material, and blending and beating equipment can produce varying textures. I implore you to use your culinary instinct at all times. Here are some further tips to help you get the best from this book:

COOK SEASONALLY

These days it is possible to buy pretty much every variety of fruit and vegetable all year round. My advice, though, is to choose your vegetables seasonally, primarily because fresh produce tastes better. Your vegetables will have ripened naturally and been harvested at the right time. They're also likely to have come from local, sustainable sources, which is better for the environment, involves less transportation, reduces the chances of spoiling and tends to be a more economical option.

MAINTAIN A WELL-STOCKED LARDER

A well-considered larder provides the building blocks for hundreds of dishes. Try to buy the best-quality ingredients that you can, as you will taste the difference.

In this book I give recipes for all sorts of homemade sauces, condiments, confits and pickles (see Chapter 11). Time allowing, I always try to make them from scratch, but they can happily be substituted with store-bought versions. Again, opt for the best quality you can buy.

Remember that store-cupboard ingredients have a shelf life. Oils will spoil over time and spices lose their pungency.

SALT & EXTRA VIRGIN OLIVE OIL

Great cooking can be very simple, requiring only a few excellent ingredients to create a spectacular dish. Salt will always be one of these ingredients, so make sure you go for a good-quality option. Flaked sea salt is best for finishing dishes, while fine salt can be used during cooking.

Extra-virgin olive oil is a little like flaked sea salt: it is brilliant for finishing dishes. It it worth having a really good bottle in your arsenal.

GRAINS & PULSES

I use grains such as bulgur, freekeh and barley frequently in my cooking. In the absence of one, or just to experiment, try swapping them.

Where possible, and time allows, I always prefer to use dried pulses that are soaked in water overnight, as they taste much better once cooked. However, we don't all have the luxury of time for forward planning. Don't be put off from trying a recipe if this is the case, simply go with the tinned variety instead, making sure they are drained and well rinsed before using.

TOASTED NUTS, SEEDS & WHOLE SPICES

Nuts and seeds are used throughout the recipes in this book and you should feel free to mix and match them in the recipes according to your tastes.

There is a marked difference in the taste and texture of a raw and a toasted nut and, unless otherwise specified, nuts should always be toasted. I tend to toast the nuts, spread evenly on a tray, in a medium-hot oven (160°C/325°F/ Gas Mark 3) for 9–10 minutes, keeping a careful eye on them and shaking them around occasionally until fragrant and golden.

Like nuts, seeds are transformed into something crunchy and aromatic when toasted. This is best done in a dry frying pan set over a medium heat. Again, keep an eye on them and move the pan regularly to ensure even colouring.

Whole spices, such as cumin, coriander or fennel also come alive once heated in a pan. They are best toasted in a dry frying pan for just a minute or two until they become fragrant.

HARISSA, CHILLI SAUCE & CHILLI FLAKES

Harissa is a wonderfully spiced North African chilli paste that can be used in many different ways: as a sauce by itself, or mixed through yoghurts, tahini sauce or mayonnaise to give an extra kick of heat. There are several brands available in supermarkets, though Belazu's Rose Harissa (which is made with rose petals) is always my go-to option.

I use other chilli sauces such as Confit Chilli Ezme (page 195) or fermented Chilli Sauce (page 195) to impart flavour and heat through my recipes and I always have a homemade bottle in my fridge. There are, however, many excellent store-bought versions, which make a perfectly good alternative.

Aleppo chilli flakes (also known as pul biber) and Urfa chilli flakes are specific types of pepper flake with distinct characteristics (Aleppo is a little fruity and Urfa a little smoky), commonly found in Turkish, Persian and Middle Eastern grocery stores. They can be substituted with regular dried chilli flakes, but do buy them if you get the chance.

LABNEH, CHEESE & EGGS

Labneh (page 191), made from yoghurt that has been strained of its whey, is used throughout this book and is easy to make yourself, but involves forward planning. It is becoming more widely available in supermarkets and local grocery stores. If you can't find it, try using crème fraîche, or Whipped Feta (page 193) instead.

This book features a wide range of different cheeses, from ricotta and manouri to goat's cheese and pecorino. It is certainly possible to swap the cheeses used in recipes, but do consider their profile when doing so and try to replace with something similar: is it crumbly, creamy or hard in texture, and delicate, mild or pungent in taste?

I would always recommend sourcing free-range, organic eggs wherever possible. Not only do they taste much better, but your money will support those implementing proper farming techniques that are better both for you and the animal. All recipes in this book that include eggs work off the assumption that they will be free-range and medium in size.

TAHINI & TAHINA SAUCE

Tahini is a raw sesame paste and the best varieties come from Lebanon, Palestine, Ethiopia and Israel. My preferred brands are S H Yaman and Al Arz.

Tahina sauce, meanwhile, is made by whipping tahini with iced water and lemon juice to aerate and thicken it (see recipe page 199). I love it. It's incredibly versatile and goes with almost everything. You can add all sorts of sauces and ingredients to tahina to change its flavour profile. A lick of harissa will add heat and colour, maple syrup will sweeten it, or it can be blended with herbs to create a vibrant green sauce.

CONFIT

I always have a few jars of confit vegetables in my fridge as they enhance dishes no end. Confit is a traditional cooking method whereby foods (in this case vegetables) are slow-cooked in liquid (in this case olive oil). If you've not tried it, it's a fantastically simple. By gently poaching them in oil, you not only preserve the vegetables, but you also intensify their flavour.

My go-tos include Confit Garlic (page 193), which provides a mellow alternative to raw garlic. They will all keep, covered in oil in an airtight container, for several weeks and in some cases much longer, and can be added to salads, sauces and sandwiches. The infused oil is a bonus and must be kept. It can be brushed, spooned or drizzled over almost anything.

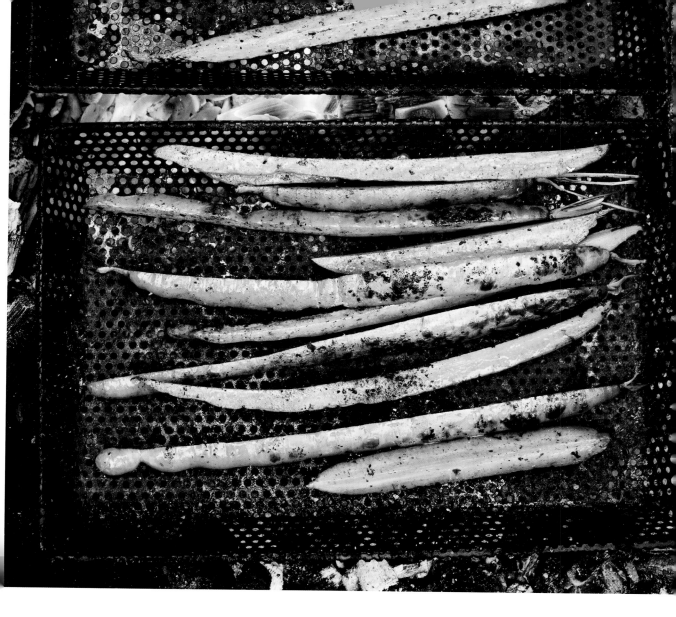

PICKLES & FERMENTS

Pickling is another excellent way of preparing and preserving vegetables. Stored properly in the fridge they keep for months and, with a nice crunch, can provide a textural contrast to dishes as well as bringing an acidic sharpness. The pickling liquor can also be used to make dressings. Some of my recipes call for the inclusion of pickles, they are not essential and you shouldn't be deterred from making the dish if you don't have it in your store cupboard.

1 RAW

RIPPED

BURRATA

With Turkish figs, hazelnuts & honey

Figs come into season towards the back end of summer, when a glut of beautifully dark, purple specimens adorn the shelves of local greengrocers and supermarkets in the UK, imported mainly from France and Turkey.

There are a number of ways to take advantage of this deluge – the humble fig is endlessly versatile – but often I find it needs little more than some good cheese and a drizzle of best-quality honey.

6 fresh Turkish figs
250g (9oz) burrata
3 tbsp floral honey, mixed
    with 1 tsp warm water
3 tbsp best-quality extra-
    virgin olive oil
50g (1¾oz) hazelnuts,
    toasted and roughly
    chopped
Picked basil leaves
Raisin or walnut bread,
    toasted, to serve
    (optional)

1 Quarter or halve the figs (or a combination of both), and lay them scattered around a plate atop and surrounding the burrata.

2 Drizzle the honey and olive oil over the plate and garnish with hazelnuts and some picked basil leaves.

3 Serve as is, or with some toasted raisin or walnut bread.

BEEF TOMATOES

With marjoram & sumac dressing

This is such a simple recipe that depends entirely on the quality of the tomato, so get the best quality that you can afford.

I like to serve these with some chunky slices of bread, brushed with olive oil, rubbed with cut garlic and dusted with some chilli flakes before going under the grill to char. Some plain toasted bread, or even no bread at all, will also suffice.

SUMAC DRESSING

100ml (3¼fl oz) best-quality extra-virgin olive oil
3 tbsp best-quality sherry vinegar
2 tsp sumac
1 tbsp pomegranate molasses
1 tsp granulated sugar
1 garlic clove, minced or grated
Flaked sea salt

BEEF TOMATOES

4 beef tomatoes, or other best-quality summer tomatoes of choice
2 small shallots, finely chopped
Handful of picked marjoram or oregano leaves
Handful of picked tarragon leaves
4–8 slices of sourdough, grilled or toasted (optional)
Flaked sea salt and ground black pepper

FOR THE SUMAC DRESSING

1 Whisk the olive oil, sherry vinegar, sumac and pomegranate molasses and sugar in a small bowl, then stir the garlic through and season with salt. Set aside to infuse for 15–20 minutes and store until required.

FOR THE BEEF TOMATOES

1 Set a deep saucepan of water over high heat and bring to the boil. Use a knife to make a small cross at the base of each tomato and blanch in the pan of boiling water for 30 seconds. Transfer immediately to a bowl filled with iced water, to stop the cooking process. Peel the tomatoes and slice horizontally into 1cm (½in) rounds.

2 Lay the tomatoes out slightly overlapping on a serving platter, season liberally with flaked salt and black pepper, and drizzle with the sumac dressing. Top the tomatoes with the chopped shallots.

3 Throw the marjoram or oregano and tarragon leaves all over the top, and serve alongside the grilled or toasted sourdough bread if you like.

CUCUMBER SALAD

With pomegranate & mint

Everybody needs a quick and easy cucumber salad to balance a barbecue menu. This pairs well with just about any protein fresh off the grill, especially fish such as salmon or trout, but also chicken. Or make it as part of a vegetarian barbecue buffet spread with Grilled Broccoli (page 56), Charred Calçots with Chermoula (page 53) and Mejaderah with Barberry and Pistachio (page 163).

5 Lebanese or baby cucumbers, cut to 3mm (1/8in) rounds

½ tbsp coarse salt, plus extra for seasoning

1 small red onion, thinly sliced

50g (1¾oz) fine bulgur

2 tbsp lemon juice

80ml (2½fl oz) extra-virgin olive oil, plus extra to finish

100g (3½oz) natural yoghurt or Greek yoghurt

1 tsp dried mint

1 tbsp pomegranate molasses

40g (1½oz) pomegranate seeds

1 red chilli, thinly sliced

Small handful of picked mint leaves

1 tbsp chopped dill

½ tsp sumac

Flaked sea salt and ground black pepper

1 Toss the sliced cucumber with the salt and set aside in a colander over the sink for 20–30 minutes.

2 Meanwhile, soak the sliced red onion in cold water for 20–30 minutes to remove some of its pungency.

3 Soak the bulgur in enough water just to cover for 5–10 minutes, drain, tip into a dry tea towel and wring dry. Transfer to a bowl and dress the bulgur with 1 tablespoon lemon juice and half the olive oil, then season to taste with salt and black pepper.

4 Combine the yoghurt, the rest of the lemon juice, 2 tablespoons olive oil and the dried mint in a small bowl and season to taste with salt and black pepper.

5 Dress the cucumber in the yoghurt dressing and leave to marinate in the fridge for at least 30 minutes.

6 Spread the dressed cucumber across a large serving plate or platter, drizzle with pomegranate molasses then top with bulgur, pomegranate seeds, drained red onion and sliced chilli. Garnish the salad with picked mint leaves and chopped dill, and finish with a dusting of sumac and drizzle of olive oil.

WINTER **FATTOUSH**

Fattoush is a Levantine salad and this is a slightly less traditional version. You can substitute the pomelo with grapefruit or blood orange. If you are unable to find Treviso, use radicchio. You could also try crumbling feta over the salad instead of whipping it.

APPLE VINEGAR DRESSING

40ml (1¼fl oz) apple cider vinegar
1 tsp Dijon mustard
1 tsp clear honey
Juice of 1 lemon
1 garlic clove, minced
120ml (4fl oz) extra-virgin olive oil
Flaked sea salt and ground black pepper

WINTER FATTOUSH

120ml (4fl oz) vegetable oil, for frying
2 pitas or flatbreads, cut into small pieces
160g (5½oz) sugar snaps, cut on the angle
3 spring onions, sliced
1 Treviso or radicchio, ripped
1 cucumber, deseeded and sliced on the angle, 1.5cm (½in) thick
1 pomelo, segmented
200g (7oz) watermelon radishes, wedged
20g (¾oz) flat-leaf parsley
120g (4½oz) Whipped Feta (page 193)
Pinch of Aleppo chilli flakes (pul biber)

TO SERVE

Handful of root vegetable crisps (optional)
Pinch of za'atar
Pinch of sumac
2 tbsp pomegranate seeds

FOR THE APPLE VINEGAR DRESSING

1 Combine the vinegar, mustard, honey and lemon juice in a small bowl and add the garlic. Set aside to infuse for several minutes before whisking in the olive oil. Season with salt and black pepper to taste.

FOR THE WINTER FATTOUSH

1 Heat the vegetable oil in a frying pan over medium heat and fry the pita pieces, making sure not to overcrowd the pan, for 3–6 minutes or until crisp and golden brown. Transfer the pita crisps to a plate lined with kitchen paper, season with salt and pepper and set aside.

2 In a large mixing bowl, combine the sugar snaps, spring onions, ripped Treviso leaves, cucumber, pomelo, radishes and flat-leaf parsley leaves and drizzle about a third of the dressing around the sides of the bowl. Toss to combine, but don't drench the salad, then season with salt and a few grinds of black pepper. If needed, add more dressing as preferred.

3 Spread the whipped feta around the perimeter of a large serving bowl and sprinkle with the chilli flakes. Place the dressed salad atop and garnish with root vegetable crisps (if using), the za'atar, sumac and pomegranate seeds. Add more dressing, if necessary, and serve immediately.

MARKET SALAD

With feta & za'atar

This salad was inspired by a recent trip to the Shuk Carmel (or market) in Tel Aviv one summer a few years back. There were huge bunches of radishes, neatly displayed tomatoes practically bursting with freshness, large piles of cucumbers lined up in exacting rows, vibrant herbs spilling everywhere and an abundance of brightly coloured exotic spices. I grabbed a handful of everything and came up with this delightfully simple recipe.

2 carrots, peeled and thinly sliced on the angle to 2mm (1/16in) thick

1 red onion, sliced as thinly as possible

4 spring onions, cut in half on the angle

2 tomatoes, cut into 6 wedges

2 radishes, very thinly sliced

1 cucumber, sliced on the angle to 1cm (½in) thick

Handful of rocket

Small bunch of chives, cut into 2.5cm (1in) batons

Soft herb leaves (such as coriander, basil, dill or mint), picked

1½ tbsp za'atar

1 tbsp dried mint

160ml (5½fl oz) Lemon Dressing (page 24)

80g (2¾oz) feta

Flaked sea salt and ground black pepper

1 Combine all the vegetables, rocket and herbs in a bowl and sprinkle the za'atar and dried mint over the top.

2 Season with salt and black pepper, spoon the lemon dressing down the side of the bowl and toss to combine. Taste and add more dressing or seasoning as needed.

3 Transfer to a serving plate and serve with a few big lumps of feta placed on top or to one side.

GRAPEFRUIT, AVOCADO & GORGONZOLA SALAD

With green beans, spinach & pecan

This is a perfectly balanced salad combining the creaminess of avocado, the citrus-sharpness of grapefruit and the piquant punchiness of gorgonzola. The roasted pecans add a warming nutty crunch. You could use macadamia or almonds instead of pecans here. Feel free to swap out the gorgonzola for something less intense such as a soft crumbly goat's cheese if blue cheese isn't your thing. When using raw onion in a salad I tend to pre-soak it in water, to reduce its pungency; it's a useful trick but optional.

HONEY-CHILLI DRESSING

50ml (1¾fl oz) red wine vinegar

2 tbsp lemon juice

1 tbsp best-quality honey

1 tsp Dijon mustard

1 shallot, finely chopped

1 tsp dried chilli flakes

150ml (5fl oz) extra-virgin olive oil

Flaked sea salt and ground black pepper

SALAD

400g (14oz) green beans

2 avocados, cut into slices or chunks

2 small red onions, thinly sliced and soaked in water for 30 minutes

200g (7oz) spinach

160g (5½oz) gorgonzola

2 grapefruits, peeled, pith removed and segmented

120g (4½oz) pecans, toasted and chopped

FOR THE HONEY-CHILLI DRESSING

1 Combine the vinegar, lemon juice and honey in a small bowl with the mustard, and add the shallot and chilli flakes. Set aside to infuse for several minutes before whisking in the olive oil. Season with salt and pepper to taste.

FOR THE SALAD

1 Blanch the green beans in boiling salted water for 2 minutes and then refresh in a bowl of water filled with ice, to stop the cooking process. Drain and set aside.

2 In a large bowl, combine the green beans, avocado, drained red onion and spinach. Drizzle with the honey-chilli dressing and toss gently. Season with salt and pepper.

3 Add the gorgonzola, grapefruit segments and pecans and gently mix through to distribute evenly.

4 Transfer to a serving plate or individual plates and serve immediately.

Serves 2 as a light main or 4 as a side dish

RAW ARTICHOKE SALAD

With fennel & rocket

There's a bit of leg-work involved with prepping artichokes; unfortunately there's just no getting away from it, but if you're willing to undertake the task, they'll reward you for your commitment.

This is a light, sharp and refreshing salad, a perfect accompaniment to Burnt Aubergine Soup (page 155) or Buttermilk-fried Cauliflower (page 180).

LEMON DRESSING
1 garlic clove, minced or grated
2 tbsp lemon juice
1 tbsp red wine vinegar
90ml (3fl oz) extra-virgin olive oil
1½ tbsp rapeseed oil
Flaked sea salt and ground black pepper

RAW ARTICHOKE SALAD
2 lemons, zested and halved
6 large globe artichokes
2 fennel bulbs, halved lengthways through the root
Handful of rocket
200g (7oz) creamy goat's cheese, ripped into small pieces
40g (1½oz) pine nuts
½ red onion, chopped
2 tbsp dill leaves
Flaked sea salt and coarse black pepper

FOR THE LEMON DRESSING

1. Combine the garlic, lemon juice, vinegar and oils in a small bowl, season generously with salt and black pepper and whisk to combine.

FOR THE RAW ARTICHOKE SALAD

1. Fill a large bowl with water and ice, squeeze the lemon halves into them and drop the halves into the bowl.

2. Cut the stems off the artichokes and the upper third (roughly 2.5cm/1in) from the top. Pull away the outer leaves to reveal the inner heart. Scoop out the hairy choke from the centre and immediately drop the artichokes into the acidulated water to prevent them from discolouring while you work.

3. Shave the cut side of each fennel half lengthways with a mandoline (or very sharp knife) as thin as possible. Drain the artichokes and do the same.

4. Toss the fennel, artichoke and rocket in a medium bowl with the lemon dressing and season with salt and black pepper. Transfer to a serving platter, dot with the goat's cheese and top with pine nuts, red onion, dill and lemon zest. Serve immediately.

WATERMELON

With ricotta salata & pine nuts

Summer holidays. Mediterranean sunshine. Long days spent by a pool doing not very much at all. Barbecues with ice-cold beer. And a huge, triangular tranche of super-sweet watermelon straight from the fridge that you gnaw to the rind. There is no finer fruit in my opinion. Because of what it represents as much as how it tastes.

This is an incredibly simple recipe that is both light and refreshing, perfect for when you're on holiday and want to make yourself lunch without it taking up too much of your precious downtime.

In the absence of ricotta salata, you could use feta, which is slightly more classic, admittedly, but for a good reason. Grilled halloumi would also be great.

1kg (2lb 3oz) watermelon, fridge-cold, rind removed and cut into chunks

2 small shallots, thinly sliced

100g (3½oz) ricotta salata, shaved

30g (1oz) pine nuts, toasted

60ml (2fl oz) extra-virgin olive oil

2 tbsp lime juice

Pinch of Aleppo chilli flakes (pul biber)

Edible flowers, such as nasturtium (optional)

2 green chillies, thinly sliced

5g (¼oz) picked mint leaves

5g (¼oz) picked basil leaves

Coarse black pepper

1 Arrange the watermelon on a serving platter and top with sliced shallots, ricotta salata and pine nuts.

2 Whisk the olive oil, lime juice and chilli flakes together and spoon over the salad. Garnish with edible flowers (if using), sliced green chillies and herbs. Finish with a few grinds of black pepper and serve immediately.

RADISH & BLACK GRAPE SALAD

With soft herbs & pistachio

Here's a simple salad for when you're in a rush but need a supporting side show for your main event. Use it to cut through a heartier and richer dish such as Hasselback Butternut Squash (page 42) or Charred Hispi Cabbage (page 52).

I tend to use soft herbs in salads. They're too often overlooked in favour of other greens and lettuces that come conveniently pre-packed, but I think they make a welcome addition to any mixed leaf combination, or indeed as a salad base, lending fragrant, peppery or anise undertones that are of interest to the palate.

2 tbsp sherry vinegar
1½ tbsp lemon juice
1 tbsp honey
2 garlic cloves, minced or grated
1 tbsp coriander seeds
60ml (2fl oz) extra-virgin olive oil
200g (7oz) radishes, trimmed and thinly sliced
2 shallots, thinly sliced
2 baby gem lettuce, leaves separated and washed
200g (7oz) black seedless grapes, cut in half
Small bunch of flat-leaf parsley leaves
Small handful of picked mint and dill leaves
1½ tsp sumac
100g (3½oz) pistachios, toasted and roughly chopped
Flaked sea salt and coarse black pepper

1 Combine the vinegar, lemon juice and honey in a small bowl. Stir in the garlic and coriander seeds, whisk in the olive oil to thicken and season with salt and black pepper to taste.

2 Combine the radishes, shallots, baby gem, grapes, herbs and sumac in a large bowl. Spoon the dressing around the edges of the bowl and gently mix the salad until the ingredients are lightly coated with the dressing. Transfer to a serving platter or bowl, garnish with the chopped pistachios sprinkled over the top and serve immediately.

2 ROASTED

SMOKED

ROASTED AUBERGINE

With marinated feta & oregano

Marinated feta is a great condiment to have in your fridge. It's paired with aubergine in this recipe but would work well with just about any roast or grilled vegetable, or indeed just by itself spread on freshly grilled bread.

Feel free to play around with the marinade ingredients. I've used seeds, hard herbs, lemon and chilli flakes in this recipe, but you could also use garlic, shallots or soft herbs (such as mint, dill or flat-leaf parsley) among many others.

MARINATED FETA
150ml (5fl oz) olive oil
1 tsp dried chilli flakes
1 tbsp coriander seeds
½ tbsp fennel seeds
10 curry leaves
250g (9oz) feta
3 lemon thyme sprigs
Pared zest of 1 lemon
2 bay leaves

ROASTED AUBERGINE
3 medium aubergines, cut
      into 2.5cm (1in) rounds
80ml (2½fl oz) extra-virgin
      olive oil
Handful of pomegranate
      seeds
30g (1oz) pine nuts,
      toasted
Oregano leaves
Flaked sea salt and ground
      black pepper

FOR THE MARINATED FETA

1 Heat half the olive oil in a small saucepan over medium heat and add the chilli flakes, coriander seeds, fennel seeds and curry leaves. Fry for 1–2 minutes, until fragrant, then remove from the heat and set aside to cool.

2 Crumble the feta into a mixing bowl, then pour over the flavoured oil and work it into the feta with your fingertips. Add the remaining ingredients strewn over the top. Cover with the remaining oil and transfer to the fridge until needed.

FOR THE ROASTED AUBERGINE

1 Preheat the oven to 220°C (425°F)/200°C Fan/Gas Mark 7.

2 Lay the aubergine slices on a roasting tray lined with parchment paper and liberally brush both sides with extra-virgin olive oil. Season generously with salt and black pepper, then roast in the oven for about 30 minutes or until golden brown.

3 Set the aubergine aside until cool enough to handle, then layer the aubergine on a serving platter or large plate, slightly overlapping each other, working around the parameter of the plate into the centre.

4 Sprinkle the feta over the top of the aubergine slices, along with any flecks of oil from the marinade, then garnish with the pomegranate seeds, pine nuts and picked oregano. Serve immediately, still warm, or at room temperature.

Serves 4–6 as a light main
or as part of a spread

SALT-ROASTED POTATOES

Salt-roasting works by drawing the excess moisture out of the ingredient being cooked and in so doing intensifying its flavour. There are different ways to salt-roast. You can encase the ingredient entirely in a salt 'crust', in which the salt is bound by water or egg white, a technique that captures most of the escaping moisture so that the vegetable (or protein) cooks evenly and gently steams within. Or you can simply roast on a bed of coarse salt granules. This recipe is a combination of both techniques, covering the potatoes as much as possible without going to the effort of encasing them in a crust.

Up to 2kg (4lb 6oz) coarse
     sea salt
8 medium baking
     potatoes, such as a
     Russet or Idaho, rinsed
     and scrubbed
3 rosemary sprigs
3 thyme sprigs
6 garlic cloves

ADDITIONAL
TOPPINGS
Extra-virgin olive oil
Sumac Yoghurt (page 190)
Harissa Crème Fraîche
     (page 191)
Confit Garlic cloves
     (page 193)
Green Tahina (page 199)
2 hard-boiled eggs, peeled
     and sliced
Confit Shallots (page 200)
Tomato and Pomegranate
     Dressing (page 189)
Pickled Guindilla Chillies,
     store-bought
Flaked sea salt and ground
     black pepper

1 Preheat the oven to 180°C (350°F)/160°C Fan/Gas Mark 4.

2 Layer the bottom of a heavy-based ovenproof casserole or saucepan with salt and place the potatoes on top, evenly spaced so that they aren't touching but still snug. Add the herbs and garlic cloves, and sprinkle the rest of the salt on top of the potatoes so that they are almost covered.

3 Roast the potatoes for 45–55 minutes, or until slightly shrivelled and completely tender, then remove from the oven.

4 Dust the salt off the potatoes and transfer to a serving plate. Gently squeeze each potato at its base so that the flesh bursts through the top skin, or split each potato open with a knife. Drizzle each potato with olive oil and sprinkle with salt and few generous grinds of black pepper. Top each potato with a generous dollop of sumac yoghurt and/or whatever alternative toppings you like. Serve baking hot ideally, but at room temperature they will still taste delicious.

TIP | Don't feel compelled to make all of the toppings here, they're merely suggestions. Pick out your favourites and make only what you can manage.

ROASTED JERUSALEM
ARTICHOKES

With labneh

Roasting Jerusalem artichokes at a higher temperature creates a lovely crisp skin that contrasts the softer creaminess of the flesh perfectly. It also brings out their natural, nutty sweetness, which makes them such a pleasurable vegetable to eat.

If you don't want to go to the effort of making your own labneh, you can use store-bought. It is often sold in Turkish and Middle Eastern stores either in a packet or as rolled balls in oil. You can always enhance labneh by whipping it with some lemon juice or zest, olive oil and perhaps a grated clove of garlic.

600g (1lb 5oz) Jerusalem artichokes, washed and scrubbed

12 garlic cloves, skin-on

2 or 3 lemon thyme sprigs

2 marjoram sprigs

60ml (2fl oz) olive oil, plus extra to finish

1 tsp Aleppo chilli flakes (pul biber)

1 tbsp honey

100g (3½oz) Labneh (page 191) or crème fraîche

30g (1oz) hazelnuts, toasted and roughly chopped

1 lemon, cut into wedges

Flaked sea salt and coarse black pepper

❶ Preheat the oven to 240°C (475°F)/220°C Fan/Gas Mark 9.

❷ Lay the artichokes on a parchment-lined baking sheet and add the garlic and herbs. Drizzle with olive oil and sprinkle with the chilli flakes and some salt and a few generous grinds of black pepper.

❸ Roast the artichokes for 15–20 minutes, shaking the baking sheet periodically, removing the artichokes when lovely and charred at the surface and just tender when pierced with a knife. Transfer to a bowl, drizzle the honey over the top, and cover with clingfilm so that the artichokes continue to steam in their own residual heat.

❹ Transfer the artichokes to a serving plate, spoon all of the juices and herbs over the top, squeeze the garlic cloves loosely out of their skins and serve alongside a large spoonful of labneh. Finish with a final drizzle of olive oil, the toasted hazelnuts strewn all over and some lemon wedges served alongside.

❺ The artichokes can be served piping hot or at room temperature.

CHILLI-ROASTED
PUMPKIN

With bulgur, soft cheese & hazelnut

We serve this dish in our restaurant every autumn. The pumpkin purée adds sweetness and moisture, but you can leave it out if you're looking to save time or effort.

Mizithra cheese is a soft Greek whey cheese that can be difficult to source. Alternatively, use a soft, crumbly goat's cheese or ricotta.

PUMPKIN PURÉE

¼ small pumpkin (approx. 300g/10½oz), peeled and cut into pieces
75g (2¾oz) brown sugar
Juice of 1 lemon
Flaked sea salt and ground black pepper

CHILLI-ROASTED PUMPKIN BULGAR

¾ small pumpkin (approx. 900g/1lb 9oz), cut into 1cm (½in) slices
60ml (2fl oz) olive oil
30g (1oz) light brown sugar
2 tbsp Aleppo chilli flakes (pul biber)
2 tbsp lemon thyme leaves
120g (4½oz) bulgur
Handful of dill and flat-leaf parsley, chopped
40g (1½oz) hazelnuts, toasted
40g (1½oz) capers, drained and rinsed
60ml (2fl oz) Lemon Dressing (page 24)
100g (3½oz) Mizithra or soft, fresh whey cheese

FOR THE PUMPKIN PURÉE

1 Set the pumpkin in a steamer over boiling water and steam for 12–15 minutes, until completely tender. Transfer to a food processor, add the sugar and lemon juice and blend until smooth.

2 Transfer the purée to a saucepan and cook over low heat for 10–15 minutes, until thickened and concentrated in flavour. Remove from the heat and set aside to cool until needed.

FOR THE CHILLI-ROASTED PUMPKIN BULGAR

1 Preheat the oven to 220°C (400°F)/200°C Fan/Gas Mark 7.

2 Roll the pumpkin in the olive oil, sprinkle with the sugar and chilli flakes and season generously with salt and black pepper. Transfer the pumpkin to a parchment-lined baking tray, scatter the lemon thyme over the top, and roast for 20-25 minutes until tender and slightly charred.

3 In the meantime, prepare the bulgur by covering it with boiling water in a small bowl and allowing it to soak for roughly 5 minutes. Drain, lightly run a fork through the grain to fluff it, so that it doesn't become clumpy, and set to one side to cool.

4 Combine the bulgur with the chopped herbs, hazelnuts and capers and stir through the lemon dressing. The tabbouleh should be light and sharp not drenched and heavy. Check for seasoning and adjust accordingly.

ROASTED
KABOCHA SQUASH

With whipped tahina, pickled fennel & crisp sage

Kabocha squash, also known as Japanese pumpkin, has a lightly speckled green exterior and an intensely sweet flesh, closer in flavour and texture to a sweet potato than a pumpkin. Look out for it in Asian grocers, or any well-stocked greengrocers. If you cannot find kabocha, you can substitute for butternut or pumpkin.

In the absence of pickled fennel, use Pickled Red Onions (page 201).

WHIPPED TAHINA

80g (2¾oz) Tahina Sauce (page 199)
2 tbsp full-fat Greek yoghurt
½ tbsp lemon juice
Flaked sea salt

ROASTED KABOCHA SQUASH

1 kabocha squash, cut into 8 wedges
80ml (2½fl oz) olive oil
1 tbsp dried oregano
1½ tbsp light brown sugar
Vegetable oil, for frying
Small handful of picked sage leaves
100g (3½oz) Pickled Fennel & Orange (page 201)
1 red chilli, finely sliced
1 ripe avocado, thinly sliced
30g (1oz) hazelnuts, roughly chopped
Flaked sea salt and ground black pepper

FOR THE WHIPPED TAHINA

1 Combine the tahina sauce, yoghurt and lemon juice in a bowl and whisk vigorously to incorporate – the consistency should be light and airy, like whipped cream. Season with salt to taste and add more lemon juice if necessary.

FOR THE ROASTED KABOCHA SQUASH

1 Preheat the oven to 220°C (425°F)/200°C Fan/Gas Mark 7.

2 Roll the squash in the olive oil, season with salt and black pepper and add the dried oregano. Transfer to a parchment-lined roasting pan, sprinkle with the light brown sugar and roast for 30–35 minutes, or until tender and charred.

3 Meanwhile, fill a deep saucepan until about a third full with vegetable oil and heat over medium heat until 180°C/350°F when probed with a thermometer. Fry the sage leaves until crisp and transfer to a tray lined with kitchen paper to absorb any excess oil. Season with salt and set aside until required.

4 Spread the whipped tahina on the base of a serving plate, using the back of a spoon. Lay the roasted squash atop and garnish with pickled fennel, red chilli, avocado and hazelnuts. Finish with the crisp sage leaves on top, a final drizzle of extra-virgin olive oil and serve.

TURLU TURLU

Turlu turlu, a Turkish version of ratatouille, has a notoriously long list of ingredients, but don't let that put you off. It's a heart-warming dish full of comfort and soul.

TOMATO SAUCE

150ml (5fl oz) olive oil
3 shallots, finely chopped
4 garlic cloves, minced
1½ tsp smoked paprika
50g (1¾oz) tomato paste
120ml (4fl oz) water
400g (14oz) tin of tomatoes
2 tbsp lemon juice
1 tbsp honey
½ tbsp pomegranate
    molasses
Sea salt and black pepper

TURLU TURLU

1 aubergine, quartered
    and cut into 3 pieces
2 courgettes, sliced into
    2cm (¾in) pieces
1 tsp salt
1 onion, thinly sliced
1 red pepper, deseeded
    and diced to 2cm (¾in)
1 green pepper, deseeded
    and diced to 2cm (¾in)
2 small carrots, peeled and
    cut into wedges
1 sweet potato, diced to
    3cm (1¼in)
100ml (3½fl oz) olive oil
4 garlic cloves, sliced
½ tbsp dried chilli flakes
1 tbsp coriander seeds
½ tsp ground allspice
½ tsp ground cinnamon
200g (7oz) cooked
    chickpeas
5g (¼oz) coriander
5g (¼oz) parsley
60g (2oz) toasted pine nuts

FOR THE TOMATO SAUCE

1 Warm the olive oil in a heavy-based saucepan over medium-low heat and cook the shallots and garlic for 5–7 minutes, until softened and translucent but not coloured. Stir in the smoked paprika and tomato paste and continue to cook for a few minutes, before adding the water and stirring to combine.

2 Add the tinned tomatoes and lemon juice, bring to a simmer and allow to cook for 20–25 minutes, until thickened and reduced. Stir through the honey and pomegranate molasses, tasting for balance (the sauce should be rich, sweet and not too acidic), and adjust the seasoning with salt and black pepper to taste. Set aside until needed.

FOR THE TURLU TURLU

1 Put the aubergine and courgettes in two separate colanders and sprinkle with the salt. Set over the sink for 20–30 minutes, to draw out the moisture, then rinse under cold water.

2 Preheat the oven to 220°C (425°F)/200°C Fan/Gas Mark 7. Toss the aubergine, onion, peppers, carrots and sweet potato together in a large bowl with the olive oil, garlic, chilli flakes, coriander seeds and spices, and season generously with salt and black pepper. Transfer to a parchment-lined roasting tray large enough to accommodate all of the vegetables comfortably in a single layer. Transfer the vegetables to the oven and roast for 45 minutes or so, gently stirring every 15 minutes, then add the courgettes and continue to cook for a further 15 minutes.

3 Warm the chickpeas through in the tomato sauce, taste for seasoning and adjust accordingly.

4 Remove the vegetables from the oven and gently fold through the chickpeas and their sauce, along with half the herbs, being careful not to break up the roasted vegetables too much. Transfer to a serving platter and garnish with the rest of the herbs, the toasted pine nuts and final drizzle of olive oil. Serve warm or at room temperature.

HASSELBACK
BUTTERNUT SQUASH

With shallot confit & walnut tarator

Hasselback is a technique for cooking potatoes originating from Hasselbacken, a restaurant in Stockholm where the dish is alleged to have been first served. The potatoes are sliced at intervals but kept connected at the base, and then roasted in clarified butter until crispy on the outside but soft and tender within. This brilliant technique works on a number of different vegetables, including swede and sweet potato, but this is a favourite.

WALNUT TARATOR

80g (2¾oz) walnuts, toasted
1 shallot, finely chopped
1 red chilli, deseeded and finely chopped
120g (4½oz) Greek yoghurt
½ bunch of coriander, shredded
20g (¾oz) sumac
Juice of ½ lemon
Flaked sea salt and ground black pepper

BUTTERNUT SQUASH

1 butternut squash, cut in half lengthways
80g (2¾oz) unsalted butter
120ml (4fl oz) olive oil
Rosemary and thyme sprigs
4 Confit Shallots (page 200)
2 tbsp toasted jasmine rice, coarsely ground
1 tbsp pumpkin seeds, toasted
Few tarragon sprigs

FOR THE WALNUT TARATOR

1 Remove the skin from the walnuts by rubbing them briskly, then chop to a medium crumb, retaining some texture.

2 Combine the chopped walnuts with the rest of the ingredients for the tarator, fold through and adjust the seasoning to taste with salt and black pepper.

FOR THE BUTTERNUT SQUASH

1 Preheat the oven to 200°C (400°F)/180°C Fan/Gas Mark 6.

2 Make incisions into each butternut squash half, at intervals of roughly 2mm (1/16in), about two-thirds of the way into the flesh and along its entire length.

3 Melt the butter in a saucepan over medium heat, add the olive oil, rosemary and thyme sprigs, and cook for a few minutes to infuse.

4 Dip and roll each squash half in the butter to generously coat. Lay the squash halves alongside the other in a cast-iron pan or roasting pan, season generously with salt and black pepper, and roast in the oven for 45 minutes to an hour, basting regularly with the excess butter mix. The squash should caramelize as it roasts and become soft and unctuous.

5 Once cooked all the way through and meltingly soft, transfer the squash to a plate and garnish with a dollop of walnut tarator, some confit shallots and sprinkle with ground toasted rice and toasted pumpkin seeds. Finish the dish with some picked tarragon leaves.

SMOKED BEETROOT
CARPACCIO

With whipped mascarpone, horseradish & granola

If you don't feel like building a fire or getting your barbecue going, you can oven-roast the beetroot instead (at 200°C/400°F/180°C Fan/Gas Mark 6), preferably on a bed of coarse salt, to draw out excess moisture and intensify the beetroot's sweetness.

The addition of granola in this recipe is a playful touch intended to add some crunch and texture. If it reminds you too much of your breakfast, you can substitute with hazelnuts, or walnuts.

This is a very simple recipe, which, as is always the case with simple recipes, depends upon the quality of the ingredients used. Try and source high-quality vinegar for this one. It will make all the difference to the dish.

8 beetroot, scrubbed
100g (3½oz) mascarpone
100g (3½ oz) sour cream
2 garlic cloves, grated
100ml (3½fl oz) extra-virgin
    olive oil
160g (5½oz) best-quality
    (or homemade) granola
4cm (1½in) piece of
    horseradish
Picked dill fronds and
    marjoram leaves
2 spring onions, finely
    sliced
Zest of 2 lemons or
    oranges, very
    finely sliced
50ml (1¾fl oz) sherry
    vinegar
Flaked sea salt and ground
    black pepper

1 Set a barbecue up for indirect grilling, with a large pile of burning embers piled to one half of the grill.

2 Place the beetroot directly on the coals and roast until the outer layer is well charred, roughly 10–12 minutes, turning regularly with a pair of tongs. Remove the beetroot from the coals, restore the grill rack and add some chunks of wood to the fire then place the beetroot on the grill rack, off-set from the burning embers, with the barbecue lid on. Smoke the beetroot for a further hour or so, until tender when pierced with a knife to the centre. Remove from the grill and set aside until cool enough to handle.

3 Meanwhile, whip the mascarpone and sour cream together in a bowl with the garlic and 2 tablespoons olive oil until smooth, and season to taste with salt and black pepper.

4 Slice the beetroot into 3mm (⅛in) rounds with a sharp knife or mandoline, leaving the skin on, and transfer to a tray.

5 Spread the mascarpone around the base of a serving plate, lay the beetroot atop and sprinkle with granola. Using a very fine grater (such as a Microplane), grate the horseradish over the top and garnish with the herbs, spring onions, lemon zest, vinegar and a very generous glug of extra-virgin olive oil.

SMOKED KOHLRABI

With sheep's cheese & sweet pepper relish

Kohlrabi is fast becoming one of my favourite vegetables to cook with. It has a creamy nuttiness similar to celeriac, a delicate but distinct flavour that pairs brilliantly with cheese, nuts and a hint of heat from a chilli flake. This is a wonderfully warming, autumnal dish that can work as a mezze for sharing or as a light starter.

Urfa chilli flakes are dried pepper flakes from the Urfa region of Turkey. They have a smoky, almost chocolate-like flavour, which is very distinctive. If you cannot find them, Aleppo chilli flakes (pul biber) or dried chilli flakes will suffice.

3 kohlrabi
300g (10½oz) rock salt (if using the oven method)
3 Turkish green chilli peppers or 2 green peppers
2 tbsp best-quality extra-virgin olive oil
Grated zest and juice of 1 lemon
1 tsp caster sugar
3 tbsp hazelnut oil
60g (2oz) whole hazelnuts (skin on), toasted and chopped
1 tbsp sesame seeds
1 tsp Urfa chilli flakes
1 tbsp picked oregano leaves
200g (7oz) semi-hard sheep's cheese such as ricotta salata, queso fresco or Tzfat cheese, to serve
Flaked sea salt and coarse black pepper

BARBECUE METHOD

1 Light a barbecue, pierce each kohlrabi several times with a skewer and place them directly onto the glowing charcoal embers. Roast the kohlrabi on the coals, turning regularly, until the outer layer is completely blackened. Transfer to the grill grate, position the opposite side of the heat source for indirect cooking, put the lid on the barbecue and add some wood chunks to the fire. Smoke the kohlrabi for 1–1½ hours until tender when pierced with a knife.

OVEN METHOD

1 Preheat the oven to 240°C (475°F)/220°C Fan/Gas Mark 9, lay the kohlrabi on a roasting tray atop a bed of salt (about 300g/10½oz) and oven-roast for 45 minutes to 1 hour, or until golden and crisp on the outside and the flesh is tender within when pierced with a knife.

2 While the kohlrabi is cooking, prepare the relish. Place the peppers on the grill (or naked flame on the stovetop) and char all over until nicely blackened and softened. Transfer to a bowl and cover with clingfilm. Leave to sit for 10–15 minutes, until cool enough to handle. Remove the peppers and peel, deseed and roughly chop the flesh, drizzle with the olive oil and lemon juice, and season with a pinch of salt and the sugar to taste.

3 Transfer the kohlrabi from the barbecue, or oven, and set aside until cool enough to handle. Peel the kohlrabi with your hands, removing the charred outer skin, cut into wedges and place on serving plates. Season generously with salt and black pepper, then drizzle with hazelnut oil and garnish with toasted hazelnuts, sesame seeds, the sweet pepper relish, Urfa chilli flakes, oregano and lemon zest. Serve with a wedge of cheese and eat immediately.

3 GRILLED

CHARRED

BURNT AUBERGINE

With tahina & smacked cucumber

This is an unusual combination of Asian and Middle Eastern flavours that happens to work perfectly. Smacked cucumber is a great salad to have up your sleeve and works as a light and refreshing side dish to cut through a heavier and rich main course.

Szechuan chilli oil can be found in just about any self-respecting Asian grocery store. If you don't have one near to where you live, you could substitute this with an alternative chilli oil.

SMACKED CUCUMBER

2 baby cucumbers
    (Lebanese), or 1 large
1 tsp salt
1 tbsp Szechuan chilli oil,
    or other chilli oil
1 tsp sesame oil
¾ tbsp soy sauce
50ml (1¾fl oz) rice vinegar
1 tsp Aleppo chilli flakes
    (pul biber)
2 garlic cloves, minced
4 tbsp crème fraîche
Pinch of sugar

BURNT AUBERGINE

4 medium-sized
    aubergines
50ml (1¾fl oz) olive oil
160g (5½oz) Basic Tahina
    Sauce (page 199)
1 tsp nigella seeds
1 tsp sesame seeds,
    toasted
5g (¼oz) coriander, finely
    chopped

FOR THE SMACKED CUCUMBER

1 Place the cucumber/s on a chopping board, lay a heavy chef's knife or meat cleaver flat on top and, with the palm of your hand, smack the knife a few times until the cucumber splits. Cut into 1cm (½in) angled slices, sprinkle with the salt and toss. Set in a colander over the sink and leave for 20–25 minutes.

2 Combine the oils, soy sauce, rice vinegar, chilli flakes and garlic in a small bowl and stir through the crème fraîche. Pour the dressing over the cucumber and set aside to marinate for a minimum of 15 minutes.

FOR THE BURNT AUBERGINE

1 Set a barbecue up for direct grilling. In the absence of a barbecue you can also use the flame from the hob. (It's a good idea to line the stovetop with foil to avoid excess mess.)

2 Pierce the aubergines 5–6 times with a knife or skewer and place on the grill rack directly over the glowing embers. Grill the aubergines, turning regularly until blackened and charred all over and soft all the way through. Remove from the heat and set aside in a colander over the sink until cool enough to handle.

3 Peel the aubergines carefully, doing the best you can to retain their original shape, while leaving the stems attached. Season the aubergines generously with salt and pepper, and drizzle with the olive oil.

4 Transfer the aubergines to serving plates and drizzle with the tahina sauce. Top each with the smacked cucumber salad, spooning any excess dressing all around. Finish with the sesame seeds and coriander sprinkled on top.

CHARRED
HISPI CABBAGE

Cabbage is one of my favourite vegetables to grill. It yields to the fire and chars beautifully, developing a far more complex flavour. You could also use Brussels sprouts. Try and make your muhammara with a pestle and mortar, as it produces a more authentic and satisfying version. Or you can use a food processor instead.

MUHAMMARA

1 garlic bulb
100ml (3½fl oz) olive oil
2 red peppers
1 banana shallot, sliced
30g (1oz) tomato paste
25g (1oz) red pepper paste
30g (1oz) sourdough, toasted and ripped into small pieces
40g (2¾oz) walnuts, toasted
½ tbsp ground cumin
½ tbsp pomegranate molasses

HISPI CABBAGE

1 green hispi cabbage, outer leaves removed, quartered
2 tbsp olive oil, plus extra to drizzle
Picked tarragon leaves
Flaked sea salt and ground black pepper

FOR THE MUHAMMARA

1 Preheat the oven to 200°C (400°F)/180°C Fan/Gas Mark 6. Slice the top 5mm/¼in off the garlic and place on a parchment-lined baking tray. Drizzle with 2 tablespoons olive oil, season with salt, and cover loosely with foil, crimping the edges slightly. Roast for 30–40 minutes, until caramelized and completely soft when gently pressed with your fingers.

2 While the garlic is cooking, place the red peppers over a naked flame on the stovetop (or barbecue) and cook until softened and nicely blackened all over. Transfer the peppers to a bowl, cover with clingfilm and set aside until cool enough to handle. Peel the peppers, deseed and roughly chop the flesh.

3 Heat 2 tablespoons oil in a small heavy-based saucepan over medium heat and cook the shallot for 5–7 minutes, until softened and translucent. Add the tomato and red pepper pastes and fry for 2–3 minutes, stirring regularly. Squeeze the garlic cloves out of their skins and transfer, along with the peppers and shallots, to a pestle and mortar. Add the toasted sourdough, walnuts, cumin and pomegranate molasses along with the remaining olive oil, and pound to a coarse, chunky paste. Season with salt and pepper to taste.

FOR THE HISPI CABBAGE

1 Prepare a large bowl of iced water. Bring a saucepan of water to the boil over high heat. Blanch the cabbage for roughly 2 minutes, until softened but still al dente, drain, then refresh it in the bowl of iced water immediately to stop the cooking process. Drain completely once cool and pat dry with kitchen paper.

2 Brush the cabbage with the olive oil and season with salt and black pepper. Prepare a barbecue for single-zone direct grilling, ensuring you are cooking over burning hot embers. Alternatively, place a ridged cast-iron skillet over high heat until smoking hot. Grill the cabbage on all sides until charred. Spread the muhammara across a serving platter, transfer the cabbage on top and drizzle with extra olive oil. Garnish with tarragon and serve immediately.

CHARRED CALÇOTS

With chermoula dressing, capers & egg

Calçots, a type of green onion closely resembling a large spring onion, derive from Spain, where they are celebrated at special festivals. They are grilled whole and then wrapped in newspaper to steam, served with romesco sauce and eaten by hand. A wonderful display of convivial, bon viveur spirit. If you don't have a newspaper you can skip this step, and simply transfer the calçots to a covered bowl to create the self-steaming effect.

As an alternative, you could use young leeks or large spring onions, but this dish would also work well with roasted or fried aubergine.

CHERMOULA DRESSING

0ml (2fl oz) olive oil

tbsp lemon juice

garlic cloves, minced or grated

0g (¾oz) coriander, finely chopped

0g (¾oz) flat-leaf parsley, finely chopped

½ tsp smoked paprika

tsp ground cumin

0g (1oz) capers, drained, rinsed and finely chopped

laked sea salt and coarse black pepper

CHARRED CALÇOTS

–10 calçots (or use young leeks)

medium-boiled eggs, peeled and roughly chopped

0g (1oz) Crispy Sourdough Breadcrumbs (page 188), optional

FOR THE CHERMOULA DRESSING

1 Combine the ingredients for the dressing in a small bowl and season to taste. Set aside.

FOR THE CHARRED CALÇOTS

1 Wash the calçots in cold running water and then soak, fully submerged in cold water, for 20–30 minutes.

2 Prepare a fire for grilling and once the embers are burning hot spread them across the base of the barbecue, forming a coal bed for the calçots. Grill the calçots directly on the embers for 8–10 minutes, turning frequently and seasoning generously with flaked salt, until tender when pierced with a knife.

3 Once cooked through, remove the calçots from the fire and wrap in newspaper to allow them to steam in their residual heat. Rub off the outer, charred layer (but don't be too concerned by removing it all) and transfer to a serving plate.

4 In the absence of a barbecue, heat a ridged cast-iron skillet pan until smoking hot and grill the calçots, turning with tongs, until charred all over and cooked.

5 Drizzle the chermoula dressing over the top, followed by the egg and, if using, sourdough breadcrumbs. Finish with a few grinds of black pepper.

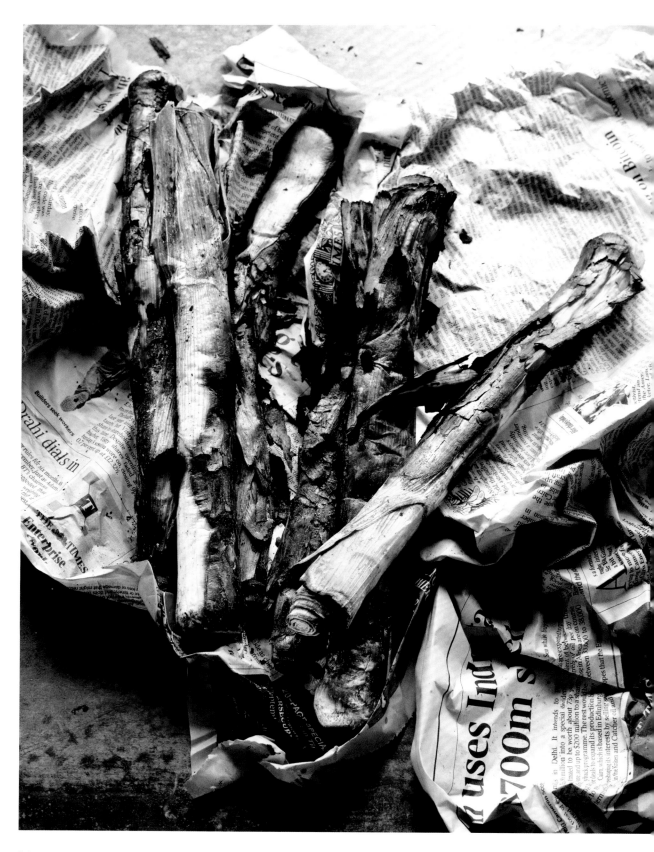

BERBER&Q: ON VEGETABLES

GRILLED BROCCOL

With pickled red onion, rose harissa & pistachio

Broccoli is a perfect vegetable for the barbecue because it has a forgiving nature and a flavour profile that really benefits from a good charring.

I'm not going to suggest building yourself a fire simply to grill off a few pieces of broccoli, especially as a cast-iron skillet heated to smoking hot on the stovetop will also work. That said, I'm not going to stop you either.

2 broccoli heads
50ml (1¾fl oz) olive oil
2 tbsp lemon juice
2 tbsp rose harissa (I like Belazu's brand) or harissa
60g (2oz) Pickled Red Onions (page 201)
Handful of pistachios, toasted and chopped
2 tbsp golden sultanas, soaked in boiling water for 15 minutes and drained
Flaked sea salt and ground black pepper

❶ Cut the broccoli through the stem to make 6–8 large 'trees' per broccoli. Trim off the woody ends but leave some stalk.

❷ Set a pan of salted water over high heat and bring to a rolling boil. Prepare a bowl filled with iced water and blanch the broccoli trees for no more than 2 minutes. Transfer with a slotted spoon to the ice bath as soon as the broccoli is al dente; it's important not to overcook the broccoli at this stage.

❸ Set a barbecue up for direct grilling, ensuring that you are cooking over hot embers. Alternatively, set a cast-iron grill pan over high heat until smoking hot.

❹ Roll the broccoli in a bowl with half the olive oil and season liberally with salt and black pepper. Grill the broccoli over high heat, on both sides, for about 2 minutes, until charred and crisped in parts. While the broccoli is grilling, combine the remaining olive oil, the lemon juice and rose harissa in a bowl and whisk to combine. Toss the broccoli with the harissa dressing and adjust the seasoning to taste.

❺ Transfer the broccoli to a plate and garnish with the pickled red onions, pistachios and golden sultanas.

GRILLED NECTARINES

With jalapeño-mint pesto, stracciatella & macadamia

The key to grilling fruit over a fire is to ensure you get your grill grate very hot. You want the nectarine to sear hard and fast, not to stew slowly, so that it chars on the outside but remains firm at its centre. Resist the urge to move the fruit too much. You want the fruit's natural sugars to burn and for the fruit to effectively unstick itself when it's ready. If you can't find stracciatella, simply substitute with burrata or mozzarella. The sourdough croutons are made using any leftover oil from Confit Garlic (see page 193), as it's a great way to avoid any waste. You can use normal olive oil instead.

JALAPEÑO-MINT PESTO

50g (1¾oz) jalapeño peppers, deseeded and chopped
25g (1oz) mint leaves, chopped
1 garlic clove, minced
120ml (6fl oz) olive oil
Grated zest and juice of 1 lemon
30g (1oz) walnuts, toasted and coarsely chopped
Flaked sea salt and ground black pepper

CROUTONS

80ml (2½fl oz) Confit Garlic oil (page 193), or use olive oil
200g (7oz) crusty sourdough, ripped into 2.5cm (1in) pieces
2 garlic cloves, skin-on and smashed

FOR THE JALAPEÑO-MINT PESTO

1 In a small bowl, combine the jalapeños, mint, garlic, olive oil and lemon zest. Fold the walnuts through the mixture. Season with salt and pepper and set aside until needed. The pesto can be kept in an airtight container for up to 3 days, though the mint will discolour and darken slightly. Bring the pesto to room temperature and stir through the lemon juice just before serving.

FOR THE CROUTONS

1 Heat the oil in a frying pan over medium heat until shimmering, then throw in the bread, making sure not to overcrowd the pan.

2 Toss the bread in the oil and cook undisturbed for 2 minutes or so, then give the croutons a turn and continue to cook until golden brown on the outside but still slightly soft and chewy in the centre, tossing them in the pan regularly as they cook. Add the smashed garlic cloves to the pan a few minutes before the end and season with salt and pepper.

3 Transfer the croutons to a tray or plate lined with kitchen paper and set aside until needed. The croutons can be made several days in advance and kept in an airtight container, where they will last for up to a week.

GRILLED NECTARINES

2 nectarines, stones
    removed and quartered
2 tbsp olive oil
Small handful of
    watercress
160g (5½oz) stracciatella
    di bufala (or burrata)
40g (1½oz) macadamia
    nuts, toasted and
    roughly chopped
Drizzle of Herb Oil (page
    190) (optional), or else
    use extra-virgin olive oil

FOR THE GRILLED NECTARINES

1 Set a barbecue up for direct grilling, or alternatively heat a ridged cast-iron skillet pan over high heat until smoking hot.

2 Roll the nectarine quarters in the olive oil and season with salt and pepper. Grill the nectarines, turning once at a 45-degree angle to create a lovely crosshatch-char mark, and then turn each piece over and repeat on the reverse side.

3 Place the watercress on a serving plate to act as a base and transfer the grilled nectarine pieces to sit atop, along with the stracciatella. Drizzle the plate liberally with the jalapeño-mint pesto, then garnish with the macadamia and the sourdough croutons. Finish with an optional drizzle of herb oil.

SMOKY AUBERGINE

With pomegranate molasses dressing & shallot salad

This is a Middle Eastern version of the Thai salad yum makeua yao (grilled aubergine salad), combining charred aubergine flesh with plenty of fresh herbs, shallots, chilli and a sweet and sour dressing to bring it all together. Toasted, ground jasmine rice adds a nutty crunch. This recipe gets 'nul points' for authenticity but a 9.8 for flavour. I offer no apologies for this bastardized concoction; you'll thank me later for it.

POMEGRANATE MOLASSES DRESSING

1 tbsp pomegranate molasses
½ tbsp tamarind concentrate
1 tbsp grape molasses (or maple syrup)
1 tbsp lemon juice
2 Confit Garlic cloves (page 193), mashed, or 1 finely chopped garlic clove
2½ tbsp olive oil
Flaked sea salt and ground black pepper

SMOKY AUBERGINE

2 aubergines
80ml (2½fl oz) olive oil
1 shallot, finely sliced
1 tbsp pomegranate seeds
Small handful of coriander leaves
Small handful of dill leaves
1 red chilli, finely sliced
½ tbsp lemon juice
2 eggs, boiled for 7 minutes then peeled and halved
½ tbsp toasted jasmine rice, ground

FOR THE POMEGRANATE MOLASSES DRESSING

1 Combine the pomegranate molasses, tamarind concentrate, grape molasses, lemon juice and confit garlic in a bowl and whisk in the olive oil to combine. Check for seasoning and adjust accordingly. Set aside until required. The dressing can be made up in advance and kept for up to 3 days but should be whisked together just prior to using.

FOR THE SMOKY AUBERGINE

1 Set a barbecue up for direct grilling. In the absence of a barbecue you can also use the flame from the hob. (It's a good idea to line the stovetop with foil to avoid excess mess.)

2 Pierce the aubergines 5–6 times with a knife or skewer and place on the grill rack directly over the glowing embers. Grill the aubergines, turning regularly until blackened and charred all over and soft all the way through. Remove from the heat and set aside in a colander over the sink until cool enough to handle.

3 Peel the aubergines carefully, doing the best you can to retain their original shape, while leaving the stems attached. Season the aubergines generously with salt and pepper, and drizzle liberally with 60ml/2fl oz olive oil. Set aside to cool to room temperature.

4 Combine the shallot, pomegranate seeds, herbs and chilli, and add the lemon juice and remaining olive oil.

5 Transfer the aubergines to a serving platter, drizzle with the pomegranate molasses dressing and serve with the shallot salad and the eggs, and finish with a sprinkling of ground-toasted rice.

GRILLED FRENCH STRING BEANS

With lemon & garlic

Grilling beans and peas is an addictive cooking technique that you will return to time and again once discovered. I've used French green beans in this recipe, but runner beans would work just as well.

This works best as a side dish. It's a lovely accompaniment to Parsnip Schnitz with confit garlic aioli (page 174).

800g (1lb 12oz) French green beans (or use regular green beans), trimmed

70ml (2¼fl oz) best-quality extra-virgin olive oil

2 tbsp grated lemon zest

Juice of 2 lemons

100ml (3½fl oz) hazelnut oil

10–12 Confit Garlic cloves (page 193), roughly chopped

bunch of chives, finely sliced

2 tbsp finely chopped dill leaves

2 shallots, thinly sliced

120g (4½oz) hazelnuts, toasted and chopped

Flaked sea salt and coarse black pepper

❶ Set a fire up for grilling over hot embers. Alternatively, heat a ridged cast-iron grill pan over high heat until smoking hot. Mix the green beans in a bowl with the olive oil until well coated, and grill over high heat, rolling them back and forth frequently, for 4–5 minutes until charred and softened but not burnt.

❷ Remove the beans from the grill and transfer to a mixing bowl. Add the lemon zest and juice, the hazelnut oil, chopped confit garlic cloves and herbs, and season generously with salt and black pepper. Give the beans a gentle mix through and transfer to a serving plate. Garnish with sliced shallots and chopped hazelnuts. Serve immediately.

CHARRED MOROCCAN CARROT SALAD

With harissa crème fraîche & saffron-candied sultanas

In Morocco, a selection of cold salads is commonly served as a starter course to any meal, accompanied by freshly baked bread, olives and harissa, and eaten in much the same way as one would eat mezze.

This carrot salad is a staple of Moroccan cuisine – steamed, diced and then dressed with little more than some best-quality paprika, olive oil and a good squeeze of lemon juice. Here is my version of this humble dish, with a few extras to add some punch, but the inspiration is very much rooted in simplicity.

4 large carrots
70ml (2¼fl oz) extra-virgin
    olive oil
Juice of 1 lemon
½ tbsp smoked paprika
1 tbsp chopped flat-leaf
    parsley
½ tbsp chopped tarragon
120g (4½oz) Harissa
    Crème Fraîche
    (page 191)
25g (1oz) Saffron-candied
    Sultanas (page 202)
1 tbsp pine nuts, toasted
2 Preserved Lemons (page
    202 or store-bought),
    rind-only, thinly sliced
Handful of picked dill
Flaked sea salt and ground
    black pepper

1 Toss the carrots in a bowl with roughly half the olive oil and season liberally with salt and black pepper.

2 Build yourself a small fire or set a barbecue up for grilling over medium heat. Alternatively, set a cast-iron pan over high heat until smoking hot. Turn your extraction fan on to full, if you have one.

3 Char the carrots until blackened all over then turn once to char the reverse side. The carrots should be tender to a knife, with a lovely blackened crust on the outside. Remove from the grill, transfer to a bowl and cover with clingfilm, to continue to steam in their own residual heat until cool enough to handle, about 5–7 minutes.

4 Dice the carrots into about 2cm (¾in) pieces, then toss in the remaining olive oil, lemon juice, smoked paprika and chopped herbs. Season liberally with salt and pepper to taste.

5 Spoon the harissa crème fraîche onto the base of a plate, add the dressed carrots on top, and garnish with saffron-candied sultanas, pine nuts and preserved lemon rind. Finish with a few dill leaves strewn all over.

TIP   You can omit the saffron-pickled sultanas and simply soak the sultanas in boiling water to soften for 15 minutes.

GRILLED SWEET POTATO

With tamarind crème fraîche & turmeric-candied nuts

You don't need to use all of the different nuts and seeds if you're missing some in your pantry. Just double up on those that you do have. Any combination would work here.

TURMERIC-CANDIED NUTS

50g (1¾oz) cashew nuts
40g (1½oz) pecan nuts
60g (2oz) macadamia nuts
40g (1½oz) pumpkin seeds
50ml (1¾fl oz) sunflower oil
½ tbsp ground turmeric
½ tbsp ground cumin
1½ tbsp runny honey
20g (¾oz) light brown sugar
2 tsp dried chilli flakes
1 tsp fine salt

TAMARIND CRÈME FRAÎCHE

150g (5oz) crème fraîche
2 tbsp tamarind concentrate
1 tbsp date syrup
1 tbsp lime juice

SWEET POTATO

3 medium sweet potatoes,
    cut into large wedges
70ml (2¼fl oz) olive oil
½ bunch of chives, sliced
3 spring onions, sliced
1 tbsp nigella seeds
2 red chillies, thinly sliced
5g (¼oz) coriander leaves
50ml (1¾fl oz) Chilli Sauce
    (page 195) or sriracha
Flaked sea salt and ground
    black pepper

FOR THE TURMERIC-CANDIED NUTS

1 Preheat the oven to 190°C (375°F)/170°C Fan/Gas Mark 5½.

2 Combine all the ingredients in a mixing bowl, except the chilli flakes and salt, and mix to combine. Transfer to a parchment-lined baking tray and roast for 15 minutes, stirring occasionally, until caramelized and dark brown. Remove from the oven and season with the chilli flakes and salt. Set aside to cool and roughly chop. Store in an airtight container until needed, where they will keep almost indefinitely.

FOR THE TAMARIND CRÈME FRAÎCHE

1 Combine all the ingredients in a medium bowl and stir to incorporate. Season with salt and black pepper to taste and set aside until needed.

FOR THE SWEET POTATO

1 Bring a large pan of salted water to the boil over high heat, carefully add the sweet potatoes, reduce to a rolling simmer and cook for about 12–15 minutes, or until just tender but not falling apart. Drain the potatoes and set aside until cool enough to handle.

2 Heat a ridged cast-iron grill pan over high heat until smoking hot or set a fire up for grilling over hot embers. Mix the sweet potato wedges with half the olive oil in a bowl, season with salt and grill over high heat on both sides for 3–5 minutes, until well scored.

3 Transfer the sweet potatoes to a serving platter, season with black pepper and top with the tamarind crème fraîche and candied nuts, then the chives, spring onions, nigella seeds, chillies, coriander leaves and chilli sauce. Finish with a drizzle of olive oil and serve immediately or at room temperature.

COAL-ROASTED VEGETABLES

With green tahina

This is the only recipe in this book for which there is no substitute or alternative cooking method and really demands the use of fire. You can of course roast each vegetable in the oven at its highest setting to circumvent the absence of outdoor space or a barbecue, but the beauty of this dish lies in its simplicity and it's just not quite the same without the kiss of some glowing embers and the unmistakable perfumed scent of smoke.

1 kohlrabi
1 red pepper
1 aubergine
1 red onion
1 sweet potato
70ml (2¼ fl oz) olive oil
Grated zest of ½ lemon
    and 1 tbsp juice
1 tbsp picked thyme leaves
1 bunch of rocket
120g (4½oz) Green Tahina
    (page 199)
1 tbsp picked oregano
    leaves
Extra-virgin olive oil, to
    serve
Flaked sea salt and ground
    black pepper

❶ Build a large fire in your barbecue and wait until the flames pull back, leaving only a bed of burning embers.

❷ Throw the vegetables directly onto the hot coals, cover them scantily with the glowing embers and char the outside of each one, turning them regularly until softened or completely tender when pierced with a knife. The vegetables will cook at different speeds, but you can pull them off and transfer them to the grill grate to rest and keep warm as and when each is ready.

❸ Transfer the red pepper to a bowl and cover with clingfilm to steam in its own residual heat. When cool enough to handle, peel and deseed, and rip the flesh into several large pieces.

❹ Repeat the process with the aubergine, kohlrabi and red onion, peeling them while still warm but cool enough to handle. Don't be too obsessional about removing all the skin as the stragglers left behind will only add a lovely smoked flavour. Drizzle with half the olive oil, throw the lemon zest and picked thyme leaves over the top and season generously with salt and a few generous grinds of black pepper. Set aside to marinate briefly while you prepare the other elements.

❺ Dress the rocket with the rest of the olive oil and the lemon juice. Spread the green tahina on the base of a serving platter. Place the rocket on top followed by the coal-roasted vegetables, and garnish with oregano. Finish with a final drizzle of olive oil and serve warm or at room temperature.

GRILLED
CORN-ON-THE-COB

With whipped labneh, preserved lemon & harissa dressing

There are many schools of thought when it comes to the best method for grilling corn-on-the-cob. My preferred method is to pre-soak your corn, peeling back the husks so as to remove the corn string first, then replacing the husks as they were and dropping the corn into a large pan of water to soak for a minimum of 15 minutes or up to 8 hours. You can then place the corn straight on the grill. The husks will form a protective layer that slowly burns off, gently steaming the corn within, working in much the same way as tin foil would.

HARISSA DRESSING

1 tsp lime juice
1 tsp ground cumin
1½ tbsp red wine vinegar
2 tbsp agave syrup (or use honey instead)
2 tbsp harissa
100ml (3½fl oz) olive oil
Flaked sea salt and ground black pepper

GRILLED CORN-ON-THE-COB

200g (7oz) Labneh (page 191)
2 tbsp olive oil
Grated zest and juice of 1 lemon
4 corn-on-the-cobs, pre-soaked, husks retained
10g (⅓oz) amba (optional)
2 tbsp finely sliced chives
2 tbsp finely chopped dill
1 tbsp za'atar
Grated zest of 1 lime
Flaked sea salt and ground black pepper

FOR THE HARISSA DRESSING

1 Combine the lime juice, cumin, vinegar, agave syrup and harissa in a medium bowl and whisk in the olive oil gradually to emulsify. Season with salt and black pepper and set aside until needed.

FOR THE GRILLED CORN-ON-THE-COB

1 Whip the labneh with the olive oil, lemon zest and juice in a medium bowl with a whisk until light and airy. Set aside until needed but don't make this too far in advance or the labneh will lose its aeration.

2 Heat a ridged cast-iron grill pan over high heat until smoking hot or set a fire up for grilling over hot embers.

3 Place the corn on the pan or grill rack, husks and all, and grill, turning regularly, for 10–12 minutes or until blackened and charred. Pull off and discard the burnt outer husks and return the corn to the grill to blacken quickly on all sides.

4 Transfer the corn to a serving platter, season with salt and black pepper and smother in whipped labneh. Spoon the harissa dressing all over the top and drizzle with amba (if using). Garnish the corn with chives and chopped dill, the za'atar and lime zest. Serve immediately while still warm.

GRILLED ASPARAGUS

With courgette tzatziki & chilli-fried lentils

I like to blanch my asparagus before grilling them, to lock in their vibrant green colour, but if you're short of time or inclination you can just grill them straight. Chilli-fried lentils are a snack in and of itself. Make a big batch and keep them back for munching on in front of the TV, or to serve alongside olives as some nibbles at your next dinner party.

COURGETTE TZATZIKI

1 courgette, peeled and thinly sliced lengthways
1 tbsp salt
200g (7oz) Greek yoghurt
1 tbsp dried mint
10g (⅓oz) dill, roughly chopped
1 garlic clove, minced
Grated zest and juice of 1 lemon
1 tbsp extra-virgin olive oil
Flaked sea salt and ground black pepper

CHILLI-FRIED LENTILS

80g (2¾oz) dried Puy lentils
200ml (7fl oz) olive oil
1 tsp ground cumin
1 tbsp flaked sea salt
10g (⅓oz) Thai red chillies, sliced into 1cm (½in) rounds
3 green chillies, sliced into 1cm (½in) rounds
3 garlic cloves, thinly sliced

GRILLED ASPARAGUS

3 bunches of asparagus, woody ends trimmed
1 tbsp olive oil
Flaked sea salt and ground black pepper

FOR THE COURGETTE TZATZIKI

1 In a medium bowl, massage the salt into the courgette well and transfer to a sieve or colander. Set aside over a sink or large bowl for an hour or so to drain, then wring the courgette in some muslin or a tea towel to squeeze out as much liquid from it as possible.

2 Transfer the courgette to a large bowl, add all of the remaining ingredients and mix through to combine. Check for seasoning and adjust accordingly, adding more lemon juice if necessary.

FOR THE CHILLI-FRIED LENTILS

1 Put the lentils in a medium saucepan, cover with at least twice the depth of salted water, bring to boil over high heat and reduce the heat to a gentle simmer. Par-cook the lentils for 12–15 minutes, until just tender but still al dente, then drain and set aside in a colander to drip dry and cool.

2 Heat the oil over medium-high heat until shimmering and fry the lentils for 5–7 minutes, or until crisp. Sift out of the oil with a spider or slotted spoon and transfer to a bowl lined with kitchen paper. Season the lentils with the cumin and flaked salt.

3 Return the oil to the heat and fry the chillies for 3–5 minutes, stirring regularly, until crisp. Use a spider or slotted spoon to remove from the oil and add to the lentils and then repeat this process with the garlic, being careful not to let it burn, another 3–5 minutes.

4 Stir the lentil mixture well to combine, and then drizzle with some of the olive oil used for frying (this will be well flavoured from the chilli and garlic), reserving any excess oil for later. You want the lentil mix to be lightly dressed in the oil, not overly heavy or greasy. Season to taste.

FOR THE GRILLED ASPARAGUS

1   Bring a saucepan of salted water to the boil over high heat and blanch the trimmed asparagus for 2 minutes, transferring to a bowl of iced water to stop the cooking process.

2   Heat a ridged cast-iron skillet pan over high heat until smoking hot, or set a fire up for grilling over hot embers. Roll the asparagus spears in olive oil and grill over high heat until charred all over, a couple of minutes on both sides, transfer to a plate or tray and season with salt and pepper.

3   Spread the grilled asparagus over the base of a serving platter, top with the tzatziki and finish with the chilli-fried lentils spooned all over. Drizzle any reserved chilli oil used for frying the lentils over the top and serve immediately.

GRILLED HALLOUMI

With pineapple ketchup & fennel salad

I don't know anybody who doesn't like grilled halloumi. There's something about its salty, rubbery texture, which, when charred over fire, becomes irresistible.

PINEAPPLE KETCHUP

150g (5½oz) pineapple
    flesh, very thinly sliced
75g (2¾oz) dried apricots
35g (1¼oz) caster sugar
50ml (1¾fl oz) cider
    vinegar
Juice of ½ lemon
1 red chilli, finely diced

FENNEL SALAD

1 fennel bulb, thinly sliced
    or shaved with a
    mandoline
½ red onion, thinly sliced
Combination of picked
    dill, mint and flat-leaf
    parsley leaves
5g (¼oz) chives, sliced into
    2.5cm (1in) batons
Pinch of sumac
Juice of ½ lemon
2 tbsp extra-virgin olive oil,
    plus extra to serve
Flaked sea salt and ground
    black pepper

GRILLED HALLOUMI

2 halloumi cheeses
    (approx. 500g/1lb2oz
    in total)
60ml (2fl oz) olive oil

FOR THE PINEAPPLE KETCHUP

1 Bring the pineapple, apricots, sugar and vinegar to the boil in a heavy-based saucepan over medium-high heat. Reduce the heat to a simmer and cook for 12–15 minutes, or until the pineapple is tender and the apricot softened.

2 Drain the fruits, reserving the cooking liquor in a cup, and transfer to a food processor. Blend the pineapple with the lemon juice and slowly add the reserved cooking liquor until completely smooth, neither too dry, nor too loose, with the consistency of mango chutney. Pass the ketchup through a sieve until smooth, then fold the red chilli through.

FOR THE FENNEL SALAD

1 Combine the fennel, red onion and herbs in a bowl. Add the sumac, lemon juice and olive oil, and stir through. The salad should be lightly coated, not wet. Season to taste with salt and pepper and add more lemon juice if needed.

FOR THE GRILLED HALLOUMI

1 Set a barbecue up for grilling over high heat directly over the burning embers. Alternatively, set a ridged cast-iron skillet over high heat until smoking hot. The grill needs to be searing hot to prevent the halloumi from sticking.

2 Unwrap the cheese and pat dry with kitchen paper. Slice each block of cheese into 4 pieces, roughly 1cm (½in) thick. Grill the halloumi for 2–3 minutes on both sides, turning 45° halfway through the cooking of both sides to form a crosshatch pattern. Resist the urge to meddle with the cheese too much. It should form a deep char mark that will naturally cause it to unstick itself from the grill when it's ready to be turned.

3 Transfer the halloumi to a serving plate, dot each piece of cheese with a dollop of pineapple ketchup and a small handful of the fennel and herb salad, then finish with an overly generous glug of olive oil around the plate.

CHARRED TENDERSTEM
BROCCOLI

With confit chilli ezme, confit garlic, almonds & yoghurt

This recipe was inspired by the now-legendary broccoli salad with chilli and garlic that I made every day during my time working at Ottolenghi. To the best of my knowledge it is still the only salad never to have come off the menu, such is its continued popularity, even after all these years. A dish of such stunning simplicity that I have used an incarnation of it in almost every kitchen I've worked in since.

I've added a yoghurt dressing in this recipe to counter the heat from the chilli, and I confit the garlic instead of frying it to add a hit of caramelized sweetness.

160g (5½oz) Greek yoghurt
2 tbsp white wine vinegar
1 shallot, finely chopped
½ bunch of chives, finely
    sliced
50ml (1¾fl oz) extra-virgin
    olive oil
400g (14oz) tenderstem
    broccoli
3 Confit Garlic cloves
    (page 193), roughly
    chopped
2 tbsp Confit Chilli Ezme
    (page 195)
2 tsp dried chilli flakes
80g (2¾oz) almonds,
    toasted and roughly
    chopped
Flaked sea salt and ground
    black pepper

❶ Combine the yoghurt, vinegar, shallot and chives in a small bowl and stir through. Whisk in 1 tablespoon olive oil and season with salt to taste.

❷ Bring a saucepan of salted water to the boil and blanch the tenderstem broccoli for 1 minute. Drain in a colander, then transfer immediately to a bowl of iced water to stop the cooking process.

❸ Build yourself a small fire or set a barbecue up for grilling over medium heat. Alternatively, set a cast-iron pan over high heat until smoking hot and, if you have one, turn your extraction fan on to full.

❹ In a bowl, toss together the broccoli and remaining olive oil, and season with salt and black pepper. Grill the broccoli for 5 minutes, or until charred and crisp on both sides, turning regularly. Transfer the broccoli back to the bowl and add the confit garlic, confit chilli ezme, chilli flakes and almonds; toss well. Season with more salt and pepper to taste.

❺ Transfer the broccoli to a serving plate, dress liberally with the yoghurt dressing over the top and serve immediately.

VARIATION   You could swap out the almonds for hazelnuts here, or Sourdough croutons (page 58) would work well too. If you don't wish to make the confit chilli ezme, try your favourite store-bought chilli sauce instead.

4 WOOD-FIRED

BAKED

Baking with dough can be a somewhat intimidating undertaking, such that many are deterred from ever even trying, which is such a shame, because it can be a lot of fun and a great pastime for those who choose to take it up.

The process of making pizza or flatbreads can, at the highest level, be a very specialized and complex skill, with years of dedicated practice and trial and error needed to perfect the technique properly.

There are seemingly so many variables at play, different techniques or ingredients to use, that indeed if you were to ask several of the leading experts in the field for their preferred method, it's probable that no two answers would be the same.

Do you use dried or fresh yeast? Strong bread flour, double-zero flour, or a combination of both? Should you use a starter (or poolish), and should it be left inside or outside the fridge, at what temperature and for how long? Do you bulk ferment the dough as a singular mass before balling it, and if so for how long, or ball it straight away and leave it to rise outside the fridge? And how long do you prove the balls before you can use them? These are just some of the many variances in baking with dough which can impact upon the final product.

But we don't all need to be experts to roll up our sleeves and give it a go. We only learn in life by making mistakes; this is par for the course, and, as with any technique and skill, we only get better at it the more we practise. Diligence, commitment and determination are some of the key traits required to master the art of successful flatbread baking. The worst that can happen is you get it wrong and have to start again. As someone far wiser than myself once said, we have nothing to fear but fear itself.

There are many amazing portable wood- or gas-fired pizza ovens available for today's customer, all capable of reaching the exceedingly high temperatures needed to achieve the leopard-spotted crust that is the hallmark of any great dough. I like the affordable Roccbox by Gozney.

PIDE & LAHMACUN DOUGH

Pide and lahmacun tend to be made from the same dough and just shaped differently. Where lahmacun is rolled out paper thin and intended to be very flat and crisp at its edges, pide is usually rolled into an oblong, with a thickened edge, forming a distinctive boat-like shape. For both, the basic dough is traditionally made with strong bread flour and yeast, with a final product that is very crisp on the outside, and compact and chewier on the inside. The dough has the added benefit of being ready to use within 3 to 4 hours.

5g (¼oz) fresh yeast
35ml (1¼fl oz) warm water
    (26–29°C/179–84°F)
½ tsp runny honey
175g (6oz) strong white
    bread flour
125g (4½oz) 00 flour
3g (⅛oz) fine salt
½ tbsp olive oil
135ml (4½fl oz) ice-cold
    water

1 Combine the fresh yeast, warm water and honey in a bowl and whisk vigorously to dissolve, roughly 30 seconds. Set aside for 10 minutes to give the yeast time to activate. The mixture should start to bubble and foam – if it does not, and the yeast granules rise to the surface instead, discard the yeast and start again with a different batch.

2 Place the flours in the bowl of a standmixer fitted with a dough hook, add the salt and olive oil and pour in the ice-cold water. Run the mixer on its lowest speed, for about minute or so, then add the yeast mixture and continue to mix on lowest speed for a further 5–7 minutes until the dough comes together as a smooth, pliable mass (it should be soft but not sticky). If the dough feels too sticky, add a little more flour and continue to mix until the correct consistency is reached. Transfer the dough to a lightly oiled bowl, cover with a damp cloth and set aside to rest for 1 hour or until the dough has roughly doubled in size.

3 Turn the dough out onto a lightly floured work surface and knead for 2–3 minutes, then form into equally weighted dough balls (approximately 85–120g/3–4½oz each). I like to use larger dough balls (110–120g/4–4½oz) for pide and smaller ones (80–100g/2¾–3½oz) for lahmacun.

4 Transfer the balls to a lightly oiled tray, roughly 5–7cm (2–3in) apart and double-wrap loosely with clingfilm. Allow to rise for 1–2 hours, or until the dough balls have roughly doubled in size. If you wish to use the dough the following day, you can refrigerate the dough balls for up to 36 hours, ensuring that they are tightly wrapped so that they do not form a skin. Remove from the fridge 2–3 hours prior to shaping and baking.

FLATBREAD DOUGH

POOLISH STARTER

150ml (5fl oz) warm water
(26–29°C/179–84°F)
½ tsp honey
3g (⅛oz) fresh yeast,
crumbled (or 1g/
1/20oz dried yeast)
150g (5½oz) strong white
bread flour

FLATBREAD DOUGH

200ml (7fl oz) cold water
150g (5½oz) 00 flour
200g (7oz) strong white
bread flour
10g (⅓oz) fine salt
5g (¼oz) olive oil, plus
extra for greasing

FOR THE POOLISH STARTER

1 **DAY 1:** Combine the warm water, honey and yeast in a bowl and whisk vigorously to dissolve, about 30 seconds. Add the flour and stir well to combine; it should be the consistency of a thick batter. Scrape the sides of the bowl down, cover with clingfilm and set aside at room temperature for 1 hour, then transfer to the fridge for between 16 and 24 hours.

FOR THE FLATBREAD DOUGH

1 **DAY 2:** Remove the poolish from the fridge and allow 30–45 minutes for it to come back to room temperature. This is your poolish.

2 Add the cold water to the poolish and mix well to combine. Place the flours in the bowl of a standmixer fitted with a dough hook and add the poolish. Run the mixer on its lowest speed, for 1–2 minutes, until the dough comes together as a smooth, pliable mass that clings to the hook. Stop the mixer, pull the dough from the hook, scraping the sides with a spatula to pick up any loose bits and pressing the dough into any unincorporated flour. Add the salt and olive oil, and continue to mix for a further 1–2 minutes until all the oil has been absorbed and the dough has come together.

3 Transfer the dough to a work surface and knead quite vigorously for at least 3–5 minutes, until smooth. It should not be too sticky (if it is, add more flour), nor be too dry (if so, add some flecks of water). Cover the dough with a damp cloth and set aside to rest at room temperature for 15–20 minutes.

4 Rub your hands with a little olive oil and gather the dough up from the sides, lifting it upwards off the work surface by 25–30cm (10–12in) and letting the dough naturally spill over at top and bottom. Return the dough from your hands to the work surface and do the same again, this time gathering the dough from top and bottom and allowing it to spill over the left and right sides.

5 Shape the dough into a large ball, pulling it back towards yourself several times, while using your hands to cup the dough in and underneath so as to create a taut, smooth and rounded surface. Transfer to a lightly oiled bowl, tightly wrap it with clingfilm and transfer it to the fridge for 16–24 hours.

6 **DAY 3:** Remove the dough from the fridge and allow it to come back to room temperature for 45–60 minutes. Transfer to a lightly floured surface and shape into dough balls, each weighing approximately 200–220g (7½oz). Transfer to a lightly floured baking sheet, with generous spacing between each ball, wrap the sheet several times tightly with clingfilm to ensure it's airtight and set aside at room temperature for 2–3 hours to prove. The dough is ready for shaping when it passes the so-called 'poke test', in which two fingers gently pushed into the surface leave a small indented mark, as opposed to it springing back.

THREE-CHEESE PIDE

With egg & salsa verde

This is a decadent pide that does your waistline no favours at all but fills you with the joys of life instead. The acidity in the salsa verde will cut through the richness.

SALSA VERDE
2 tsp Dijon mustard
Juice of 1 lemon
1 tbsp sherry vinegar
120ml (4fl oz) extra-virgin
    olive oil
Large handful of flat-leaf
    parsley, mint and
    tarragon, chopped
2 garlic cloves, minced
40g (1½oz) capers, rinsed
    and roughly chopped
Flaked sea salt and coarse
    black pepper

CHEESE SAUCE
75g (2¾oz) unsalted butter
75g (2¾oz) plain flour
750ml (25½fl oz) milk
75g (2¾oz) cheddar,
    grated
75g (2¾oz) parmesan,
    grated
90g (3oz) halloumi, grated

PIDE
½ quantity of master pide
    dough recipe (page 79),
    rolled into 3 balls, each
    weighing 100–120g
    (3½–4½oz) (page 81)
Plain flour, for dusting
3 egg yolks
2 tbsp melted butter
1½ tbsp za'atar
Extra-virgin olive oil

FOR THE SALSA VERDE

1 Combine the mustard, lemon juice and vinegar in a small bowl and slowly whisk in the olive oil to thicken. Add the remaining ingredients and stir to combine. Season with salt and black pepper. Set to one side until required.

FOR THE CHEESE SAUCE

1 Melt the butter in a heavy-based saucepan over medium heat and whisk in the flour to form a roux. Gradually pour in the milk, roughly 100ml (3½fl oz) at a time, whisking continuously to combine. Turn the heat down to medium-low and simmer the sauce for 10–15 minutes until thickened, then fold through the cheeses and season with salt to taste. Set aside, kept warm, until required.

FOR THE PIDE

1 If you own a pizza oven or wood oven, preheat it to between 350–400°C (660–750°F). Alternatively, preheat your oven to its highest possible setting and place a pizza rack on the middle shelf or use a large, rimless baking tray.

2 Lightly flour a work surface and roll each ball (see page 80) to an oval shape, about 35 x 15cm (14 x 6in). Spread the cheese sauce down the length of the pides, leaving a 2.5cm (1in) edge along the border, using a spoon to indent a small well in the middle so as to accommodate the egg yolk. Fold the sides of the pides inward, crimping the dough firmly at each end.

3 Dust a pizza peel with some flour and very carefully transfer the pides onto the peel. Alternatively, use a flat, dusted or parchment-lined baking sheet instead. Bake the pides for 3–4 minutes in a pizza (or wood) oven, or 6–8 minutes in a standard oven, rotating the pides 180° halfway through cooking. Bake until golden brown and crisp around its edges. A minute or so before the pides are finished, crack the egg yolks into the well, turn 180° degrees and return it to the oven until golden brown and crisp around its edges.

4 Remove the pides from the oven and brush the edges with melted butter. Sprinkle with za'atar and flaked salt, then dollop the salsa verde all over and finish with an indulgent final drizzle of olive oil. Slice and serve immediately.

SWISS CHARD PIDE

With three onion, sultana & ricotta

Here is a carefully balanced pide, with sweetness from the caramelized onion and candied sultanas, a hit of vinegary sharpness from the pickled red onion, a pinch of heat from the chilli flakes and some earthy goodness from the Swiss chard. The ricotta binds it all together, though you could use a soft, crumbly goat's cheese if you prefer.

tbsp olive oil, plus extra
    for the chard
small onions, sliced
garlic cloves, sliced
50g (1lb 11oz) Swiss
    chard, stems removed
    and sliced, leaves torn
tbsp picked lemon
    thyme leaves
quantity of master pide
    dough recipe (page 79),
    rolled into 3 balls, each
    weighing 100–120g
    (3½–4½oz) (page 81)
lain flour, for dusting
20g (4½oz) ricotta
tsp Aleppo chilli flakes
    (pul biber)
tbsp melted butter
0g (2oz) Saffron-candied
    Sultanas (page 202)
0g (1oz) Pickled Red
    Onion (page 201)
tbsp grated lemon zest
½ tbsp mint leaves, finely
    shredded
spring onions, green
    parts only, finely sliced
xtra-virgin olive oil
laked sea salt and coarse
    black pepper

1 If you own a pizza oven or wood oven, preheat it to between 350–400°C (660–750°F). Alternatively, preheat your oven to its highest possible setting and place a pizza rack on the middle shelf or use a large, rimless baking tray.

2 Heat the olive oil in a deep, wide saucepan over medium-low heat and add the onion, garlic and Swiss chard stems. Cook slowly, stirring occasionally, for 35–40 minutes, or until deep golden brown. Add the thyme leaves, and season to taste with salt and black pepper.

3 Add a drizzle of olive oil to a frying pan and cook the Swiss chard leaves over medium-high heat for 1–2 minutes, until wilted. Season with salt and pepper.

4 Lightly flour a work surface and roll each dough ball (see page 80) to an oval shape, about 35 x 15cm (14 x 6in). Spread the caramelized onion down the length of the pides, leaving a 2.5cm (1in) edge along the border. Top with the Swiss chard, ricotta and chilli flakes. Fold the sides of each pide inward (see page 80), crimping the dough firmly at each end to ensure the pides hold together while cooking.

5 Dust a pizza peel with some flour and very carefully transfer the pides onto the peel. Alternatively, in the absence of a pizza peel you can use a flat, dusted or parchment-lined baking sheet instead.

6 Bake the pides for 3–4 minutes in a pizza (or wood) oven, or 6–8 minutes in a standard oven, rotating the pides 180° halfway through cooking to ensure even cooking. Remove from the oven and brush the edges of the pide with melted butter. Scatter the soaked sultanas over the top, drizzling the syrup across the pide as you do and garnish with pickled red onion, lemon zest, mint and the spring onions. Finish with a final pinch of flaked salt and a drizzle of extra-virgin olive oil. Serve immediately, piping hot, either whole or cut into segments as preferred.

SLOW-ROASTED TOMATO & CONFIT GARLIC FLATBREAD

With marjoram & chilli oil

Here is a simple flatbread that is so much more than the sum of its parts. Use the best cherry tomatoes you can find for this one – they'll make all the difference. Some Confit Cherry Tomatoes (page 194), or even Confit Shallots (page 200), would also be a welcome addition. You can play around with the herbs, too. I've used marjoram on this occasion, but basil, lemon thyme or rosemary, or a combination of all three, would also be great.

1 x master flatbread dough recipe (page 81), rolled into 4 balls, each weighing 200–225g (7–8oz)

Plain flour, for dusting

400g (14oz) best-quality cherry tomatoes, cut in half

16 Slow-roasted Tomatoes (page 194)

12 Confit Garlic cloves (page 193), roughly chopped

1 small red onion, thinly sliced

120ml (4fl oz) chilli oil from Confit Chilli Ezme (page 195) or store-bought chilli oil

Picked marjoram (or oregano) leaves

2 tbsp za'atar

Flaked sea salt

1 If you own a pizza oven or wood oven, preheat it to between 350–400°C (660–750°F). Alternatively, preheat your oven to its highest possible setting and place a pizza rack on the middle shelf or use a large, rimless baking tray.

2 Dust a pizza peel with some flour and transfer the stretched flatbread dough balls onto the peel. Alternatively, in the absence of a pizza peel, use a flat, flour-dusted or parchment-lined baking sheet.

3 Evenly scatter the cherry tomato halves over the dough followed by the slow-roasted tomatoes and confit garlic, flecked with the respective oils from both, leaving a 2.5cm (1in) border around the edge. Distribute the red onion around and season with flaked salt.

4 Bake the flatbread for 3–4 minutes in a pizza (or wood) oven, or 6–8 minutes in a standard oven, until golden brown and crisp at the edges. Turn the flatbread 180° halfway through cooking to ensure even coloration.

5 Transfer the flatbreads to a chopping board, brush the rim with any garlic oil from the confit garlic and drizzle the chilli oil over the top. Sprinkle the flatbreads with picked marjoram and za'atar. Slice and serve immediately, still piping hot.

WILD MUSHROOM & GOAT'S CHEESE FLATBREAD

With pomegranate molasses & pumpkin seeds

This is a wonderful autumnal flatbread that depends on the quality of the mushrooms. Choose the freshest and most vibrant looking available. You can opt for larger mushrooms too, such as a flat or portobello, but I would slice and cook these first with some garlic, before throwing them on the flatbread dough to go in the oven.

1 x master flatbread dough recipe (page 81), rolled into 4 balls, each weighing 200–225g (7–8oz)

Plain flour, for dusting

160g (5½oz) crème fraîche

400g (14oz) mixed wild mushrooms, (such as chanterelle, trompette or chestnut, ripped or sliced if large)

3 garlic cloves, peeled

80ml (2½fl oz) olive oil

200g (7oz) soft goat's cheese

2 tsp dried chilli flakes

2 tsp dried oregano

2 tsp roughly chopped rosemary

4 tbsp pumpkin seeds, toasted

4 tbsp pomegranate seeds

2 tbsp pomegranate molasses

Flaked sea salt and coarse black pepper

1 If you own a pizza oven or wood oven, preheat it to between 350–400°C (660–750°F). Alternatively, preheat your oven to its highest possible setting and place a pizza rack on the middle shelf or use a large, rimless baking tray.

2 Dust a pizza peel with some flour and transfer the stretched flatbread dough balls onto the peel. Alternatively, in the absence of a pizza peel, use a flat, flour-dusted or parchment-lined baking sheet.

3 Spread the crème fraiche in a thin layer from the middle of the flatbread bases towards the edge, leaving a 2.5cm (1in) border around the edge.

4 Place the wild mushrooms in a bowl, grate the garlic cloves over them, toss with the olive oil and season generously with flaked salt and black pepper. Distribute the mushrooms evenly across the flatbread rounds and crumble the goat's cheese on top, leaving a 2.5cm (1in) border still around the edge.

5 Bake the flatbreads for 3–4 minutes in a pizza (or wood) oven, or 6–8 minutes in a standard oven, until golden brown and crisp at the edges. Turn the flatbreads 180° halfway through cooking to ensure even coloration.

6 Transfer the flatbreads to a chopping board, scatter the chilli flakes, dried oregano, rosemary, pumpkin seeds and pomegranate seeds on top, and drizzle with pomegranate molasses. Finish with a light sprinkling of flaked salt, a few generous grinds of black pepper and final drizzle of olive oil. Slice and serve immediately while piping hot.

ASPARAGUS
& SPINACH FLATBREAD

With feta & green chilli

I've used spinach in this recipe, but some Tuscan kale (cavolo nero) would make a good alternative. The asparagus could be replaced with very thinly sliced courgette, or even Brussels sprouts. Play around with your flatbread toppings. The combinations are practically endless. A drizzle of truffle oil, added right at the end, would be a luxurious final touch.

1 x master flatbread dough recipe (page 81), rolled into 4 balls, each weighing 200–225g (7–8oz)

Plain flour, for dusting

160g (5½oz) crème fraîche

300g (10½oz) baby spinach leaves, washed

10 asparagus, trimmed of woody end and thinly shaved with a vegetable peeler

2 green chillies, thinly sliced

50g (1¾oz) feta, crumbled

4 eggs

8 Confit Garlic cloves (page 193), roughly chopped

Small handful of fresh basil leaves

Flaked sea salt and ground black pepper

1 If you own a pizza oven or wood oven, preheat it to between 350–400°C (660–750°F). Alternatively, preheat your oven to its highest possible setting and place a pizza rack on the middle shelf or use a large, rimless baking tray.

2 Dust a pizza peel with some flour and transfer the stretched flatbread dough balls onto the peel. Alternatively, in the absence of a pizza peel, use a flat, flour-dusted or parchment-lined baking sheet.

3 Spread the crème fraîche in a thin layer from the middle of the flatbread bases towards the edge, leaving a 2.5cm (1in) border around the edge. Distribute the spinach over the dough, followed by the thinly shaved asparagus and sliced chilli, leaving a small gap in the centre of the flatbreads in which to slide an egg. Scatter the crumbled feta all over and season with flaked salt and a few generous grinds of black pepper.

4 Bake the flatbreads for 3–4 minutes in a pizza (or wood) oven, or 6–8 minutes in a standard oven, until golden brown and crisp at the edges. Turn the flatbread 180° halfway through cooking and crack each egg into a small ramekin. Gently slide it into the gap in the middle to cook for the final few minutes until cooked through.

5 Transfer the flatbreads to a chopping board, scatter with confit garlic, season with more salt and scatter the picked basil leaves over the top to wilt in the residual heat. Slice and serve immediately, still piping hot.

PUMPKIN & RICOTTA
BOUREKAS

Bourekas are a popular stuffed Israeli pastry that can be found in all different shapes and sizes. I've used puff pastry for this recipe, but filo or even brik can also be used.

OLIVE TAPENADE

160g (5½oz) black olives, pitted
1 tbsp capers, drained and rinsed
2 garlic cloves, grated
1 tbsp chopped flat-leaf parsley
1 tsp red wine vinegar
2 tbsp olive oil

PUMPKIN & RICOTTA BOUREKAS

800g (1lb 12oz) pumpkin, peeled and cut into large chunks
50ml (1¾fl oz) olive oil
½ tsp fine salt
1 tbsp sugar, to taste (optional)
1½ tsp Aleppo chilli flakes (pul biber)
160g (5½oz) ricotta, crumbled
Grated zest of 1 lemon
500g (1lb 2oz) store-bought all-butter puff pastry
2 eggs
2 tbsp milk
10g (⅓oz) nigella seeds
10g (⅓oz) sesame seeds
Flaked sea salt and coarse black pepper

FOR THE OLIVE TAPENADE

1 Combine all of the ingredients in a food processor and pulse to a coarse paste. Transfer to a jar and set aside until required. The tapenade can be made well in advance and will keep in the fridge for up to 3 days.

FOR THE PUMPKIN & RICOTTA BOUREKAS

1 Preheat the oven to 200°C (400°F)/180°C Fan/Gas Mark 6. Spread the pumpkin out in a roasting tin, drizzle with 2 tablespoons olive oil and season with the salt. Cover with foil and roast for about 1 hour, until completely tender, stirring the squash occasionally. Remove from the oven and set aside to cool.

2 Transfer the pumpkin to a medium saucepan, crush it with the back of a fork to a coarse purée along with the rest of the oil, sugar (if using) and chilli flakes. Set the pan over medium heat and cook for 2–3 minutes, stirring continuously, just to draw out any remaining moisture. Remove from the heat and fold through the ricotta and lemon zest. Check for seasoning, adding more salt and pepper if necessary, then set aside in the fridge to cool.

3 Roll the puff pastry dough out on a lightly floured work surface into two square sheets, roughly 30cm (12in) wide and 3mm (⅛in) thick. Cut each sheet into nine 10cm (4in) squares, making 18 in total. Whisk the eggs with the milk and a pinch of salt, then brush two adjacent sides of each pastry square with the egg wash, reserving the excess for later.

4 Spoon a couple of heaped teaspoons of the pumpkin and ricotta mix into the middle of each square, then fold the side of the dough that has not been egg washed over, from corner to corner, to make a triangle. Gently press the sides together with your fingertips around the perimeter of the filling.

5 Carefully transfer the bourekas to a parchment-lined baking sheet and refrigerate for at least 30 minutes or up to 24 hours. When ready to bake, remove the bourekas from the fridge, brush the top of each one with the reserved egg wash and sprinkle with the nigella and sesame seeds. Bake in the oven for 20–25 minutes, until golden-brown, puffed and crisp. Set aside to cool slightly and serve, still warm with the olive tapenade alongside.

BUTTERNUT SQUASH LAHMACUN

This is not a traditional lahmacun topping in any sense, but it makes for a great lunch or light snack, especially if you top with the rocket salad and wrap the whole thing up.

BUTTERNUT SQUASH PURÉE

2 small butternut squash
80ml (2½fl oz) olive oil
6 small shallots, halved, skins on
3 tbsp maple syrup
4 lemon thyme sprigs
6 garlic cloves, smashed with skin on

BUTTERNUT LAHMACUN

½ quantity of master lahmacun dough recipe (page 79), rolled into 4 balls, each weighing 85–100g (3–3½oz)
Plain flour, for dusting
1½ tbsp Urfa chilli flakes
1 small red onion, thinly sliced
2 red chillies, thinly sliced
60g (2oz) rocket
60ml (2fl oz) olive oil, plus extra for drizzling
Juice of 1 lemon
60ml (2fl oz) melted butter
80g (2¾oz) pecorino, grated
4 tbsp sunflower seeds, toasted
4 tbsp pumpkin seeds, toasted
Flaked sea salt and coarse black pepper

FOR THE BUTTERNUT SQUASH PURÉE

1 Preheat the oven to 200°C (400°F)/180°C Fan/Gas Mark 6. Split the butternut squash lengthways and scoop out the seeds. Roll the squash in half the olive oil, season with salt and black pepper, and transfer to a parchment-lined baking sheet, flesh-side down. Roast in the oven for about 30 minutes, or until the flesh is just starting to brown and caramelize.

2 In a small bowl, toss the shallots with the rest of the olive oil and the maple syrup, and season with salt and pepper. Flip the butternut squash over and add the shallots on top, along with the maple syrup dressing. Throw the lemon thyme and garlic cloves on top and continue to roast the squash for a further 45 minutes, or until everything is completely tender.

3 Scoop out the flesh of the butternut squash, shallots and garlic from their skins and transfer to a food processor. Blend to a purée, check for seasoning and adjust accordingly. Set aside until required. The purée can be made up to 5 days ahead of time and refrigerated if needed.

FOR THE BUTTERNUT LAHMACUN

1 If you own a pizza oven or wood oven, preheat it to between 350–400°C (660–750°F). Alternatively, preheat your oven to its highest possible setting and place a pizza rack on the middle shelf or use a large, rimless baking tray.

2 Lightly flour a work surface and roll the dough balls (see page 80) to your preferred shape, be it a 20cm (8in) round or 25 x 15cm (10 x 6in) oval. Once shaped, place on a baking sheet lined with parchment paper and cover with a damp tea towel. Leave to rest for 30–45 minutes.

3 Dust a pizza peel with some flour and very carefully transfer the lahmacun onto the peel. Alternatively, in the absence of a pizza peel you can use a flat, dusted or parchment-lined baking sheet instead.

4 Spread the butternut squash purée across the base of the dough, leaving 1cm (½in) around the edge, and sprinkle with Urfa chilli flakes. Carefully slide the lahmacun onto the pizza stone or preheated baking tray.

5 Bake the lahmacun for 3–4 minutes in a pizza (or wood) oven, or 6–8 minutes in a standard oven, until golden brown and crisp at the edges. Turn the lahmacun 180° halfway through cooking to ensure even coloration.

6 A few minutes before the lahmacun is cooked, toss the red onion, chilli and rocket in a small bowl with the olive oil and lemon juice, and season to taste.

7 Remove the lahmacun from the oven to a chopping board and brush the edges with melted butter. Top with the grated pecorino and toasted seeds, and give a final drizzle of olive oil. Transfer to serving plates and serve immediately with the rocket salad atop, or alongside if wrapping.

LEEK & MUHAMMARA
LAHMACUN

With chilli yoghurt

Man'oushe, or manakish, is a Lebanese flatbread, very similar in composition to a lahmacun, often topped with za'atar, cheese, ground lamb or spinach, though I've also had it with muhammara as a base. It is the inspiration for this recipe.

CHILLI YOGHURT

160g (5½oz) Greek yoghurt

1½ tbsp Aleppo chilli flakes (pul biber)

¾ tbsp dried mint

Juice of 1 lemon

Fine sea salt

LEEK LAHMACUN

80ml (2½fl oz) olive oil

2 leeks, finely sliced and rinsed between layers

½ quantity of master lahmacun dough recipe (page 79), rolled into 4 balls, each weighing 85–100g (3–3½oz)

Plain flour, for dusting

240g (8½oz) Muhammara (page 52)

120g (4½oz) red peppers, sliced

2 tbsp melted butter

50g (1¾oz) walnuts, toasted and roughly chopped

Extra-virgin olive oil, for drizzling

Flat-leaf parsley leaves

Flaked sea salt

FOR THE CHILLI YOGHURT

1 Combine the yoghurt with the chilli flakes, dried mint and lemon juice in a medium bowl. Stir to incorporate and season with salt to taste.

FOR THE LEEK LAHMACUN

1 If you own a pizza oven or wood oven, preheat it to between 350–400°C (660–750°F). Alternatively, preheat your oven to its highest possible setting and place a pizza rack on the middle shelf or use a large, rimless baking tray.

2 Heat the olive oil in a heavy-based pan and cook the leeks over medium-low heat, stirring occasionally for 20–25 minutes, until softened and lightly caramelized. Season with salt and set aside.

3 Lightly flour a work surface and roll the dough balls (see page 80) to your preferred shape, be it a 20cm (8in) round or 25 x 15cm (10 x 6in) oval. Once shaped, place on a baking sheet lined with parchment paper and cover with a damp tea towel. Leave to rest for 30–45 minutes.

4 Dust a pizza peel with some flour and very carefully transfer the lahmacun onto the peel. Alternatively, in the absence of a pizza peel you can use a flat, dusted or parchment-lined baking sheet instead. Spread the muhammara across the base of the dough leaving 1cm (½in) around the edge. Top with the leeks and peppers and season with flaked salt. Carefully slide the lahmacun onto the pizza stone or preheated baking tray.

5 Bake the lahmacun for 3–4 minutes in a pizza (or wood) oven, or 6–8 minutes in a standard oven, until golden brown and crisp at the edges. Turn the lahmacun 180° halfway through cooking to ensure even coloration. Transfer the lahmacun from the oven to a chopping board and brush the edges with melted butter, then drizzle the chilli yoghurt on top followed by the walnuts. Finish with some extra-virgin olive oil and a sprinkle of flat-leaf parsley leaves. Slice and serve immediately, still piping hot.

GALETTE OF COURGETTE

With manouri cheese & chilli-honey dressing

A simple, light galette that is perfect for a summer lunch or as part of a spread at your
next garden party. Serve with a fresh, zesty mixed leaf salad and away you go.

HILLI-HONEY
RESSING

tbsp honey

tbsp lemon juice

red chilli, blackened,
    peeled and chopped

tbsp extra-virgin olive oil

aked sea salt and ground
    black pepper

ALETTE

00g (7oz) mascarpone

00g (3½oz) crème fraîche

rated zest of 1 lemon

garlic cloves, grated

50g (9oz) shop-bought
    all-butter puff pastry,
    cut and rolled to make
    two 30 x 20cm (12 x
    8in) rectangles, 3mm
    (⅛in) thick, each cut in
    half to make 4 smaller
    rectangles

egg yolk

00g (3½oz) manouri
    cheese

-2 large courgettes, very
    thinly sliced

tsp thyme leaves

tbsp olive oil

FOR THE CHILLI-HONEY DRESSING

1 Put the honey, lemon juice and chilli in a small bowl and slowly whisk in the
olive oil. Season with salt and black pepper to taste.

FOR THE GALETTE

1 Preheat the oven to 180°C (350°F)/160°C Fan/Gas Mark 4. Line a baking sheet
with parchment paper.

2 Combine the mascarpone, crème fraîche, lemon zest and garlic in a bowl, and
whisk until smooth. Season with salt and black pepper to taste.

3 Place the pastry rectangles on the lined baking sheet and brush the egg yolk
around the border of the pastry, roughly 2cm (1¼in) in from the edge. Prick the
centre gently with a fork, 5 or 6 times for each square.

4 Smear the mascarpone mix in the centre of each, crumble the manouri
cheese over it, and arrange the courgette slices on top, overlapping them
slightly. Sprinkle over a little thyme, salt and pepper, and a drizzle of olive oil.
Transfer to the oven and bake for 20–25 minutes until the pastry is golden
brown, puffed at the edges and the base is crisp.

5 Slide the galettes onto serving plates and drizzle liberally with the chilli-honey
dressing. Serve immediately while still warm.

5 SEARED

SAUTÉED

GREEN SHAKSHUKA

With swiss chard & spinach

Shakshuka, a North African dish in origin of eggs braised in a rich tomato and red pepper sauce, has become increasingly popular over the years. It's brilliantly simple and soothing and can be justifiably made at almost any time of the day. In recent times I've come to think of shakshuka less in terms of its tomato base and more as eggs cooked in a pan with any combination of random ingredients that I may have in my fridge.

The key to any shakshuka, red, green or otherwise, is to cook your eggs with the lid on, rather than baking them in the oven, so that they steam, leaving you with cooked whites and runny yolks. In short, don't overcook the eggs.

60ml (2fl oz) extra-virgin olive oil
200g (7oz) Swiss chard, stalks and leaves separated, stalks chopped, leaves roughly torn
2 small banana shallots, finely chopped
2 garlic cloves, thinly sliced
100g (3½oz) spinach
4 eggs
50g (1¾oz) Green Harissa (page 198)
40g (1½oz) Greek yoghurt
20g (¾oz) pomegranate seeds
½ tbsp pine nuts, toasted
Few coriander leaves
Flaked sea salt and ground black pepper
Grilled sourdough or pita breads, to serve

1 Warm the olive oil in a heavy-based saucepan that has a lid over medium-low heat and cook the chard stalks, shallots and garlic for 7–10 minutes, or until soft and translucent. Add the chard leaves and spinach and cook for 4–5 minutes, just until they begin to wilt. Season with salt and black pepper.

2 Make four small wells in the pan and crack an egg into each one, being careful not to break the yolk. If you do, don't worry, just carry on regardless. Season the eggs, cover the pan with the lid and cook for 3–5 minutes, or until the egg whites are just cooked through and the yolks are still runny.

3 Dot the green harissa and yoghurt around the pan, sprinkle the pomegranate seeds and pine nuts over the top and garnish with picked coriander leaves.

4 Finish with an obligatory drizzle of olive oil and serve piping hot, with grilled sourdough or pita bread.

Serves 2 as a
starter or light
main

BLACKENED TOMATOES

With ricotta & pistachio pesto bruschetta

Charring tomatoes takes a bit of practice and involves holding your nerve: resist the temptation to move them too soon. You want a dark char to form on the surface and for the tomatoes to unstick themselves from the pan when ready. This technique works well for onions and shallots as well as certain fruits, such as apricots, plums and peaches.

The pistachio pesto makes more than you need. The excess can be used to bring some flavour to your grilled vegetables or as a spread for your sandwiches.

PISTACHIO PESTO

2 garlic cloves, minced
20g (¾oz) pistachios, toasted
20g (¾oz) toasted pine nuts
15g (½oz) flat-leaf parsley leaves, chopped
15g (½oz) mint leaves, roughly chopped
100ml (3½fl oz) olive oil
Grated zest of 1 lemon
30g (1oz) freshly grated parmesan
Flaked sea salt and coarse black pepper

BRUSCHETTA

4 thick slices of sourdough
120ml (4fl oz) olive oil
500g (1lb 2oz) plum tomatoes, halved
1½ tbsp pomegranate molasses
1½ tbsp lemon juice
100g (3½oz) ricotta
4 Confit Garlic cloves (page 193)
200g (7oz) Confit Cherry Tomatoes (page 194), optional
Oregano and thyme leaves

FOR THE PISTACHIO PESTO

1 Combine the garlic, pistachios and pine nuts in a food processor and blend to a coarse and chunky paste. Add the herbs and olive oil and pulse a few times to combine; the pesto should be slightly chunky and not too smooth. Fold through the lemon zest and parmesan, and season to taste with salt and freshly ground black pepper. Set aside until needed.

FOR THE BRUSCHETTA

1 Heat a ridged cast-iron grill pan over high heat until smoking hot. Brush the sourdough slices on both sides with 2 tablespoons olive oil and grill until well scored, turning at a 45° angle halfway through to create a crosshatch pattern. (Alternatively, you can toast the bread until crisp if you prefer.)

2 Combine 50ml (1¾fl oz) olive oil with the pomegranate molasses and lemon juice in a small bowl and whisk to combine. Season with salt and black pepper.

3 Heat a heavy-based cast-iron pan over high heat until smoking hot. Brush the cut-side of tomato halves with the remaining olive oil and place them cut-side down on the hot surface. Char the tomatoes for 3–5 minutes, resisting the urge to move them. They will form a thin black crust and unstick themselves once ready to be lifted from the pan. Transfer the tomatoes to a tray using a spatula, spoon the dressing over the top while still piping hot and set aside.

4 Spread the ricotta on the base of each slice of bread and top with the burnt tomato halves and confit garlic and cherry tomatoes. Garnish with a heaped tablespoon of pistachio pesto per serving, a drizzle of any leftover dressing that has collected on the tray and the picked herbs. Serve immediately.

SEARED CARROTS

With walnut & lovage pesto, saffron yoghurt

Saffron yoghurt is a brilliant sauce to have up your sleeve. Its bright colour intensifies with time, adding a splash of vibrancy when drizzled over anything. Try it with aubergine, tenderstem broccoli or butternut squash for riotous displays of colour.
Lovage makes for a great pesto, gremolata, dressing or herb oil. It can be hard to find so you can always substitute with flat-leaf parsley or carrot tops.

25ml (¾fl oz) red wine
   vinegar
1 tbsp honey
90ml (3fl oz) extra-virgin
   olive oil
12 medium carrots, peeled
1 large shallot, thinly sliced
100g (3½oz) rocket
30g (1oz) pomegranate
   seeds

WALNUT & LOVAGE
PESTO
60g (2oz) walnuts, toasted
2 garlic cloves, grated
20g (¾oz) basil leaves
20g (¾oz) lovage leaves
   (or flat-leaf parsley)
30g (1oz) parmesan,
   grated
70ml (2¼fl oz) olive oil
Flaked sea salt and ground
   black pepper

SAFFRON YOGHURT
Pinch of saffron strands
2 tbsp boiling water
120g (4½oz) Greek yoghurt
1 garlic clove, minced
1 tbsp lemon juice
1 tbsp olive oil

FOR THE WALNUT & LOVAGE PESTO

1 Combine the walnuts and garlic in a food processor and pulse. Add the basil, lovage leaves and parmesan, and pulse to a coarse paste. Pour in the olive oil gradually, with the blade running, until incorporated, and season with salt and black pepper to taste.

FOR THE SAFFRON YOGHURT

1 Combine the saffron strands and boiling water in a small bowl and set aside to infuse for 10–15 minutes. Add the remaining ingredients to the bowl, and whisk to stir through. Check for seasoning and adjust accordingly.

FOR THE SEARED CARROTS

1 Combine the vinegar and honey in a small bowl and whisk in 60ml (2fl oz) olive oil to emulsify. Season with salt and a few grinds of black pepper.

2 Cut the carrots lengthways into quarters and toss in a bowl with the rest of the olive oil. Heat a large cast-iron grill pan over high heat until smoking hot and sear the carrots, cut-side down, until well charred and almost burnt. Turn the carrots with a pair of tongs to sear on all sides and transfer to a serving platter. Season generously.

3 Toss the shallots and rocket in a small bowl with the dressing and transfer to a serving platter. Place the seared carrots on top and drizzle with saffron yoghurt and the walnut pesto. Garnish with pomegranate seeds scattered over the top.

BROAD BEANS

With eggs, dill & turmeric butter

I often feel like life is just too short to bother with skinning broad beans. It's not compulsory to do so here. It will taste delicious regardless, though skinning them does give the dish a wonderful vibrant green colour, where leaving them as they come yields a somewhat less colourful affair. The choice, as is often the case in cookery, is yours.

200g (7oz) frozen broad
    beans
50ml (1¾fl oz) olive oil
1 medium onion, thinly
    sliced
4 garlic cloves, finely
    chopped
1 tsp ground cumin
1 tsp chilli flakes
5g (¼oz) dill
3 eggs
50g (1¾oz) unsalted butter
1 tsp ground turmeric
3 tbsp lemon juice
40g (1½oz) Greek yoghurt
Flaked sea salt and ground
    black pepper

TO SERVE
1 lemon, cut into wedges
Grilled pita breads
    (optional)

❶ Bring a large pan of salted water to the boil and blanch the broad beans for 2–3 minutes until they float to the surface, then drain and refresh under cold water or in a bowl filled with iced water. Remove the beans from their skins and set aside (see introduction).

❷ Heat the olive oil in a 30cm (12in) non-stick frying pan that has a lid and add the onion. Cook over medium-low heat, stirring occasionally, for 7–10 minutes or until caramelized. Add the garlic, cumin and chilli flakes, and cook for a further 2–3 minutes or until fragrant but not burnt. Now throw in the podded broad beans and half the dill, season with salt and black pepper, mix well and cook, stirring continuously, for a few more minutes.

❸ Make three small wells in the pan and crack an egg into each one, being careful to try not to break the yolk. If you do, don't worry, just carry on regardless. Season the eggs, cover the pan with the lid and cook for 3–5 minutes, or until the whites are cooked through but the yolks remain runny.

❹ While the eggs are cooking, melt the butter in a small saucepan over medium heat, whisking until nutty brown in colour, then add the turmeric and lemon juice and immediately remove from the heat to stop the butter from burning.

❺ Transfer the eggs from the heat, dot the yoghurt all around, drizzle the turmeric butter over and top with the remaining dill. Serve immediately, with lemon wedges for squeezing over the top and some grilled bread as an optional extra.

SEARED OKRA

With red pepper & pine nuts

The key to cooking okra is to use a high heat for searing hard and fast. This helps to tenderize the flesh while minimizing its slimy consistency, so often a deterrent for okra sceptics. Use the widest pan you own, so as to not overcrowd the okra, and cook in batches if need be.

2 red peppers
70ml (2¼fl oz) extra-virgin olive oil, plus extra to serve
1 red onion, finely chopped
400g (14oz) okra, trimmed and cut on the angle into 2cm (¾in) pieces
2 garlic cloves, minced or grated
1 tsp ground cumin
25g (1oz) Kalamata olives, pitted and halved
40g (1½oz) pine nuts, toasted
2 tbsp red wine vinegar
150ml (5fl oz) vegetable stock
60g (2oz) raisins
5g (¼oz) basil
½ tbsp Aleppo chilli flakes (pul biber)
1 tsp light brown sugar
Flaked sea salt and ground black pepper

1 Blacken the red peppers on a barbecue grill, or directly over the gas flame on the stovetop, until charred and softened. Transfer to a bowl, cover with clingfilm, and set aside for 10–15 minutes until just cool enough to handle. Peel, quarter and deseed the peppers, removing any remaining white membrane, then cut the peppers into small dice and set aside until needed.

2 Warm half the olive oil in a heavy-based, wide frying pan over medium-high heat and cook the onion for 5–7 minutes, stirring occasionally, until coloured. Remove the onion from the pan and transfer to a bowl.

3 Wipe the pan clean, add the remaining olive oil, and place back over high heat. Once the oil is just about smoking, add the okra and sear hard and fast for 3–4 minutes, until coloured, moving the pan or stirring the contents regularly to ensure an even coloration.

4 Reduce the heat to medium, add the caramelized onion back to the pan, along with the diced red peppers, garlic, ground cumin, olives and pine nuts and continue to cook for a further 1–2 minutes, stirring continuously. Pour in the vinegar, scraping any sticky bits off the base of the pan, then stir in the stock, followed by the raisins, and allow to reduce for 5–7 minutes until you have a thickened sauce. Season the okra with salt and freshly ground black pepper and stir through the basil, chilli flakes and light brown sugar to dissolve. Taste the okra; it should be just the right balance of sweet, sour and salt so adjust accordingly if needed.

5 Transfer to a serving plate, drizzle with extra olive oil and serve piping hot or still warm, preferably with some rice or creamy polenta.

TIP — Substitute the Kalamatas for any other olive. I encourage using the best-quality versions and avoid ones from a tin, which aren't good for anything.

6 STUFFED

SKEWERED

WILD MUSHROOM
KEBAB

With porcini tahina & crispy shallots

This is undoubtedly a more time-consuming recipe. It's not that it's particularly complicated, but there are a series of steps. Trust me, the reward justifies the effort.

PORCINI TAHINA
1 bouquet garni
30g (1oz) dried porcini
    mushrooms
3 dried chillies
4 garlic cloves, smashed
120g (4½oz) tahini paste
Juice of 1 lemon
1 tsp salt

MUSHROOM GLAZE
60ml (2fl oz) soy sauce
50ml (1¾fl oz) balsamic
    vinegar
30g (1oz) caster sugar
1 tbsp pomegranate
    molasses
½ tbsp date syrup

MUSHROOM KEBAB
500g (1lb 2oz) shiitake
    mushrooms, cleaned
500g (1lb 2oz) oyster
    mushrooms, cleaned
6 spring onions, cut into
    5cm (2in) batons
Olive oil, for brushing
40g (1½oz) Crispy Shallots
    (page 200)
2 Cos or butter lettuce,
    leaves separated
Mint and coriander leaves
Flaked sea salt

FOR THE PORCINI TAHINA

1 First, make the mushroom stock. Combine the bouquet garni, dried porcini, 750ml (25½fl oz) water, chillies and garlic in a saucepan and bring to the boil over high heat. Reduce the heat and simmer for 30–40 minutes, until the stock has reduced by half. Strain and reserve the stock, mushrooms and the garlic.

2 Put the porcini mushrooms and garlic from the stock in a food processor with the tahini and lemon juice. Blitz to combine; it will thicken to a coarse paste. Gradually pour in 120ml (4fl oz) of the reserved mushroom stock, blitz to incorporate and season with salt to taste. Set aside.

FOR THE MUSHROOM GLAZE

1 Combine 250ml (8½fl oz) of the reserved mushroom stock, the soy sauce, vinegar, and sugar in a saucepan. Place over medium-high heat and bring to the boil, then reduce the heat and simmer for 8–10 minutes, or until reduced by half. Whisk through the pomegranate molasses and date syrup and remove from the heat. Set aside.

FOR THE MUSHROOM KEBAB

1 Prepare a grill for direct grilling over hot embers, or heat a ridged cast-iron grill pan until smoking hot. Thread the mushrooms and spring onions on the skewers, alternating intermittently, brush with olive oil and season with salt.

2 Grill the mushroom skewers over high heat, close to the coals (if using) and brush the mushrooms with the glaze as they cook. Turn the skewers as the mushrooms cook, continuing to glaze them throughout, until softened and cooked through but slightly charred. Remove the mushrooms from the heat and set to one side on a tray to rest. Give the mushrooms a final lick of oil, sprinkle with crispy shallots and serve alongside the porcini tahina, lettuce and herbs for making little wraps with.

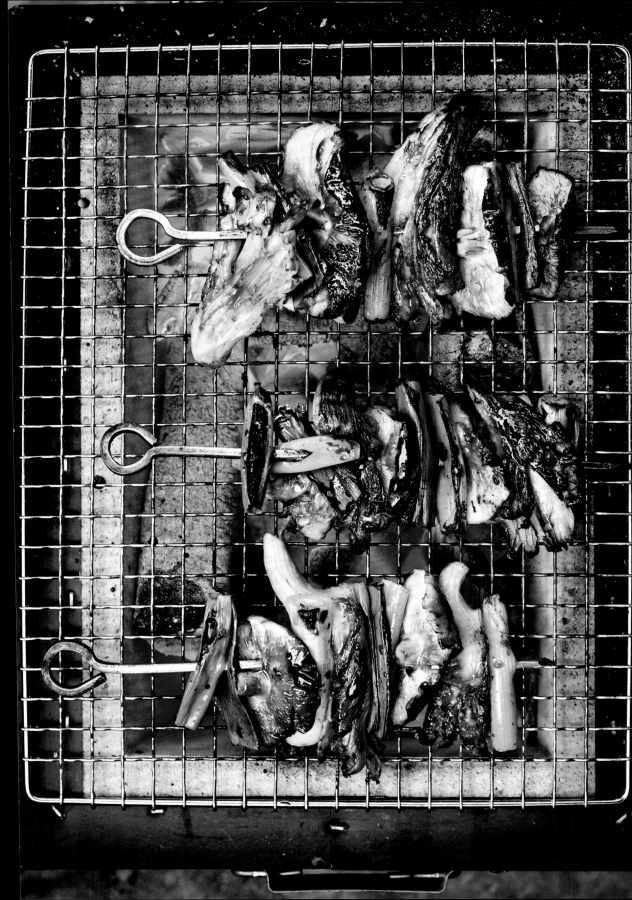

SWISS CHARD, SPRING ONION & FETA ARAYES

With sumac yoghurt

Arayes derive from Lebanon, a dish of pita bread stuffed with beef or lamb mince that has been flavoured with tomato, onions and spices and then grilled. Served with tahina sauce, they are highly addictive.

Baharat can be bought at most supermarkets and Turkish grocery stores these days. It's essentially a warm spice mix, typically always containing sweet spices such as nutmeg, clove and allspice.

120ml (4fl oz) olive oil

1 small red onion, finely chopped

500g (1lb 2oz) Swiss chard, stalks diced, leaves shredded

4 spring onions, sliced

2 garlic cloves, minced

1 tsp baharat or ½ tsp ground nutmeg with a pinch of ground clove

1 tsp ground cumin

400g (14oz) frozen spinach, thawed

100g (3½oz) feta, crumbled

160g (5½oz) mozzarella, grated

1 tbsp Aleppo chilli flakes (pul biber)

30g (1oz) pine nuts, toasted

4 pita breads

Flaked sea salt and ground black pepper

220g (8oz) Sumac Yoghurt (page 190), optional

1 Heat half the olive oil in a large heavy-based frying pan over medium heat and add the red onion, Swiss chard stalks and spring onion. Cook for 7–10 minutes, until softened and translucent. Add the garlic and spices and continue to cook, stirring frequently, for a further 2–3 minutes. Remove from the heat, season with salt and black pepper, and transfer to a large mixing bowl.

2 Squeeze the thawed spinach to remove as much liquid from it as possible and roughly chop. Add the spinach along with the shredded chard leaves, feta, mozzarella, chilli flakes and pine nuts to the bowl with the onion mixture, and give it all a good stir to ensure everything is well combined.

3 Cut each pita bread in half and stuff each pocket with the Swiss chard mixture.

4 Heat the rest of the olive oil in a frying pan over medium heat and fry the stuffed pitas, turning regularly, for 3–4 minutes, or until golden brown on all sides and the cheese is oozing. Transfer to a plate, pile high and serve accompanied by the sumac yoghurt, if using.

CAULIFLOWER
SHAWARMA KEBAB

With rose harissa tahina, pickled red onions & pine nuts

This is a new take on an old classic, our cauliflower shawarma, which has firmly established itself as our signature dish at Berber & Q. I skewered the cauliflower for this recipe, turning it into a kebab of sorts, garnished with sauces, pickles and bread.

¼ tbsp ground cumin
½ tsp ground turmeric
tbsp lemon juice
garlic clove, chopped
100g (3½oz) unsalted
  butter, softened
whole cauliflower,
  broken into florets
red pepper, cut into
  2.5cm (1in) squares
red onion, cut into 2.5cm
  (1in) squares
0g (¾oz) picked dill
  leaves
0g (¾oz) chives, cut into
  1cm (½in) lengths
0g (¾oz) picked flat-leaf
  parsley leaves
Olive oil, for tossing
laffa or flatbreads, grilled
tbsp pomegranate
  molasses
60g (5½oz) Rose Harissa
  Tahina (page 199)
0g (1oz) pine nuts,
  toasted
tbsp pomegranate seeds
0g (2¾oz) Pickled Red
  Onions (page 201)
Flaked sea salt and ground
  black pepper

1 Whisk the cumin, turmeric, lemon juice, garlic and softened butter together in a small bowl until thoroughly incorporated and set aside at room temperature.

2 Bring a large saucepan of salted water to the boil over high heat and gently drop the cauliflower florets into the pan. Bring the water back to the boil, then turn the heat down to medium so the water has a gentle roll. Parboil the cauliflower for 4–5 minutes, until just tender when pierced with a knife but not overcooked, then remove with a slotted spoon and place on a cooling rack over a roasting pan to drip-dry and cool.

3 Once cool enough to handle, thread the cauliflower florets intermittently with the red pepper and red onion, onto the skewers.

4 Set a barbecue up for single-zone direct grilling. In the absence of a barbecue or outdoor space, you can use a ridged cast-iron grill pan heated until smoking hot. Brush the cauliflower kebab with the turmeric-spiced butter and grill, basting with the butter intermittently, until well charred on both sides and the onion and red pepper are just cooked through. Season with salt and a few grinds of black pepper.

5 Toss the herbs in a small bowl with some olive oil and season to taste. Transfer the cauliflower kebab to serving plates atop the grilled laffa bread. Drizzle with pomegranate molasses and rose harissa tahina, and garnish with pine nuts, pomegranate seeds and pickled red onions. Serve immediately, while piping hot, with the herb salad alongside.

AUBERGINE SABICH SANDO

I've visited Israel on countless occasions now, mainly for its food, in search of ideas and inspiration. My first port of call when I arrive in Tel Aviv is almost always Sabih Frishman on Frishman Street, for sabich. It's become something of a first-day ritual for me. To my mind they make the best sabich in town, and it feels like I've tried most of them now. This sabich is almost nothing like the one at Sabih Frishman. This is my take on the dish, and I wouldn't dare try and replicate something as perfect as their rendition.

CURRY MAYONNAISE
120g (4½oz) mayonnaise
1 tbsp curry powder
½ tsp ground turmeric
Juice of ½ lemon
Flaked sea salt and ground
    black pepper

AUBERGINE SABICH
2 ripe tomatoes, deseeded
    and diced
1 small cucumber,
    deseeded and diced
2 spring onions, sliced
2 tsp lemon juice
1 tbsp olive oil
Vegetable oil, for frying
2 aubergines, cut into
    2.5cm (1in) rounds
4 large eggs
4 brioche or challah rolls,
    lightly toasted or grilled
4 tbsp S'chug (page 198)
1 small packet of ready-
    salted crisps
40g (1½oz) Pickled Red
    Onions (page 201)
Flat-leaf parsley leaves
Flaked sea salt and ground
    black pepper

FOR THE CURRY MAYONNAISE

1 In a small bowl, combine the mayonnaise, curry powder, turmeric and lemon juice. Check for seasoning and adjust accordingly.

FOR THE AUBERGINE SABICH

1 Combine the tomatoes, cucumber, spring onions, lemon juice and olive oil in a small bowl. Season to taste.

2 Pour enough oil to come up the sides of a deep saucepan by 1–1.5cm (½–1in) and set over medium until hot (roughly 180°C/350°F if you have a thermometer probe to hand). Fry the aubergines for 7–10 minutes, turning halfway through cooking, until golden brown on both sides. Make sure you don't overcrowd the pan and, if needs be, fry the aubergines in batches. Transfer the aubergines using a slotted spoon to a bowl lined with kitchen paper and season with salt and black pepper. Using the same pan from frying the aubergines, and any remaining oil, fry the eggs sunny-side up, and season with salt and pepper.

3 Spread some curry mayonnaise onto the base of each brioche bun and top with the aubergine slices, followed by the s'chug, then gently slide the egg on top. Add the crisps on top of the egg and finish with the pickled red onions, flat-leaf parsley leaves and a generous heaped spoon of the salad. Place the remaining bun half on top and serve immediately with the yolk from the egg oozing out the side.

STUFFED ONIONS

With freekeh & apricot

I feel like stuffing onions might be the vegetarian version of being a fishmonger. It can be a messy affair, and nobody comes out smelling any better for it. But, as with all crafts founded on technique and care, the end result justifies the effort.

100ml (3½fl oz) olive oil

2 large shallots, chopped

3 garlic cloves, chopped

¼ tsp ground allspice

½ tsp ground coriander

Pinch of ground nutmeg

200g (7oz) freekeh, rinsed
  and soaked in cold
  water for 30 minutes

Grated zest of 1 orange

60g (2oz) pine nuts,
  toasted

100g (3½oz) dried apricots,
  finely chopped

800ml (27fl oz) vegetable
  stock

3 tbsp lemon juice

10g (⅓oz) flat-leaf parsley,
  finely chopped, plus
  extra to garnish

4 large onions, peeled

2 tbsp tamarind paste

2½ tsp sugar

1 cinnamon stick

160g (5½oz) Greek yoghurt

2 mint sprigs, finely
  shredded

Flaked sea salt and ground
  black pepper

1 Warm half the olive oil in a large, heavy-based frying pan over medium-high heat and cook the shallot and garlic, stirring regularly, for 5–7 minutes, or until softened but not coloured. Add the spices and stir to combine, frying for a couple of minutes until aromatic.

2 Drain the freekeh, add to the pan and stir well to ensure the grains are coated in the spiced oil. Fold through the orange zest, pine nuts and dried apricots, add 500ml (17fl oz) of stock and bring to the boil over high heat. Reduce the heat to a very gentle simmer and continue to cook the freekeh for 35–45 minutes, until almost all of the liquid has been absorbed and the freekeh is tender (add more stock to the pan if it looks a bit dry). Season to taste, stir in the lemon juice and fold through the flat-leaf parsley. Transfer the freekeh to a tray and spread it out to cool down while you prepare the onions.

3 Trim the ends of each onion and make an incision along the length, from top to root, so you can remove a thin wedge. Bring a pan of salted water to the boil and blanch the onions for about 20 minutes, or until just tender – the layers will start to separate cleanly from each other. Refresh the onions in a bowl filled with iced water, then drain and separate the layers, setting the outer ones to one side and reserving the small inner layers for an alternative use.

4 Spoon roughly 1–1½ tablespoons of freekeh onto one half of each layer of onion and fold the other side over, rolling it up tightly so that the onion wraps around itself at least once, making an oblong shape of sorts that's slightly fatter at its centre and tapers slightly towards either end. Arrange the onions in a wide frying pan with a lid, side-by-side to fit snugly.

5 Combine the tamarind paste, remaining stock, sugar and cinnamon stick in a bowl and mix well. Season with ½ teaspoon flaked salt and pour over the onions. Put a lid on the pan, bring to a gentle simmer and reduce the heat to low. Cook the onions for about an hour, or until most of the liquid has evaporated but there remains a residual glaze-like sauce. To serve, spread the yoghurt on a plate, top with stuffed onions and drizzle the excess sauce all around. Garnish with flat-leaf parsley and mint.

THREE-CHEESE
TOASTED SANDWICH

I'm pretty sure a toasted cheese sandwich was the very first dish I ever learnt to cook. My parents owned (and still own) one of those old-school sandwich toasters that were idiot-proof, and I'd go to town on deep-filled toasted cheddar sandwiches. This recipe is a little more complicated than my early-years renditions, and far more indulgent too.

POACHED QUINCE

2 quince
500ml (17fl oz) water
300g (10½oz) caster sugar
1 star anise
1 cinnamon stick
2 cardamom pods

THREE-CHEESE SANDWICH

100g (3½oz) unsalted butter
50g (1¾oz) plain flour
500ml (17fl oz) whole milk, warmed
200g (7oz) pecorino, grated
160g (5½oz) mature cheddar, grated
40g (1½oz) Dijon mustard
2 tbsp Worcestershire sauce
8 thick slices of sourdough
120g (4½oz) taleggio (or Gruyère), thinly sliced
60g (2oz) Confit Chilli Ezme (page 195)
2 tbsp olive oil
Flaked sea salt and ground black pepper

FOR THE POACHED QUINCE

1. Peel, core and quarter the quince, and immediately drop them directly into a bowl of water with a squeeze of lemon to stop the quince from discolouring.

2. Combine the water, sugar and spices in a saucepan and bring to a simmer over medium heat for 2–3 minutes, until the sugar dissolves. Drop the quince into the pan, return to a gentle simmer and poach for 30–40 minutes, or until the quince are tender but not overcooked. Remove from the heat and allow to cool to room temperature. Set aside until required.

FOR THE THREE-CHEESE SANDWICH

1. Melt half the butter in a medium saucepan over medium heat and whisk in the flour to make a roux. Add the warmed milk gradually, whisking to remove any lumps, and cook for 5 minutes to a thick but pourable béchamel sauce.

2. Fold the pecorino into the béchamel, stirring to incorporate, then add the cheddar. Once both cheeses have melted into the sauce, add the Dijon mustard followed by the Worcestershire sauce, and check and adjust the seasoning with salt and black pepper. Set aside to cool.

3. Spread the cheese béchamel across four slices of sourdough, followed by the taleggio slices. Spread the confit chilli ezme on the opposing sourdough slices, then carefully fold over to form sandwiches.

4. Melt the remaining butter and olive oil in a heavy cast-iron grill pan, and toast the sandwiches on both sides, until a crunchy golden-brown crust has formed on the bread, and the cheese sauce is oozing within. Serve piping hot, with the quince on the side.

GRILLED VEGETABLE
SKEWER

With tahina & s'chug

This is a remarkably simple recipe. Get your sauces made up the day before and you can have this on the table in less than 20 minutes. Play around with the vegetables in the recipe by all means, but keep in mind that cooking times will vary. At the risk of patronizing you by pointing out something obvious, whatever you do choose to put on your skewer, they all need to take roughly the same amount of time to cook through. Avoid aubergine for this one. And halloumi too. We're not in the 1990s anymore.

red peppers, each cut
   into 8 pieces
onions, peeled and
   each cut into 8 pieces
   through the root
00g (14oz) cherry
   tomatoes, (roughly
   16 tomatoes, two per
   skewer)
Turkish green chilli
   peppers
00ml (3½fl oz) olive oil
20g (4½oz) Basic Tahina
   Sauce (page 199)
lemons, cut in half
tbsp S'chug (page 198)
laked sea salt and ground
   black pepper

O GARNISH
few picked coriander
   leaves, to garnish
Pinch of Aleppo chilli
   flakes (pul biber)
thyme sprigs (optional)

1 Set a barbecue up for single-zone direct grilling, ensuring you are cooking over hot embers. In the absence of a barbecue or outdoor space, you can use a ridged cast-iron grill pan heated until smoking hot.

2 Thread the vegetables onto two skewers intermittently. I like to start with a red pepper, and follow with a piece of onion, a cherry tomato and a Turkish chilli pepper. I then repeat this before finishing with a piece of red pepper, but the order is entirely up to you. Brush each skewer liberally with olive oil on both sides and season generously with salt and black pepper.

3 Grill the vegetables over the embers, turning regularly, until slightly charred and cooked all the way through.

4 Place a large spoon of tahina sauce on each plate and lay the vegetable skewer on top. Give each portion a good squeeze of lemon (reserving some lemon for cutting into wedges for each plate) and drizzle the s'chug over the top. Garnish each plate with a few picked coriander leaves, a pinch of Aleppo chilli flakes and, if using, a lemon thyme sprig.

RED PEPPER & FRIED AUBERGINE BURGER

Many moons ago while studying in Sydney I worked in a gourmet burger joint called Burger Man. This was their only vegetarian option and it was to die for. Sadly, Burger Man is no longer around, but its legacy lives on through this recipe.

GARLIC-BASIL MAYO
1 bunch of basil
3 garlic cloves
160g (5½oz) mayonnaise
Juice of ½ lemon
Flaked sea salt and black pepper

RED PEPPER & FRIED AUBERGINE BURGER
2 small beetroot
80g (2¾oz) rock salt or coarse sea salt
2 red peppers
90ml (3fl oz) olive oil
1 aubergine, cut into 8 rounds
1½ tsp table salt
Vegetable oil, for frying
1 parsnip, peeled and shaved into ribbons
1 tsp ground cumin
1 bunch of rocket
1 tbsp lemon juice
120g (4½oz) Whipped Feta (page 193)
4 brioche burger buns, toasted
2 pickled cucumbers, thinly sliced

FOR THE GARLIC-BASIL MAYO

1 Combine the basil, garlic and mayonnaise in a food processor and blend until smooth. Add the lemon juice and pulse. Check and adjust the seasoning.

FOR THE RED PEPPER & FRIED AUBERGINE BURGER

1 Preheat the oven to 180°C (350°F), 160°C Fan, Gas Mark 4. Rinse and scrub the beetroot to remove excess dirt and pat dry with kitchen paper. Make a bed of coarse salt in a shallow roasting tin and arrange the beetroot on top. Roast in the oven for approximately 1½ hours until tender (to test, pierce each one with a knife. You should be able to reach the centre easily but still with just the slightest of resistance). Once cooked, remove from the oven and set aside until cool enough to handle, then peel and slice into 1cm (½in) thick rounds.

2 While the beetroot are roasting, blacken the red peppers on a barbecue grill, or directly on the gas flame on the stovetop, until charred and softened. Transfer to a bowl, cover with clingfilm and leave to cool. Peel, quarter and deseed the peppers, removing any remaining white membranes. Place in a bowl and drizzle over 2 tablespoons olive oil. Set aside until needed.

3 Toss the aubergine slices in the table salt and place in a colander set over a sink for 45 minutes. Rinse under running water and squeeze dry. Pour enough oil to come up the sides of a wide, shallow frying pan by 2.5cm (1in) and set over medium heat until hot (roughly 180°C/350°F). Fry the aubergine slices for 5–7 minutes, turning halfway, until golden brown on both sides and completely tender. Use a slotted spoon to transfer the aubergine to a bowl lined with kitchen paper and season with flaked salt.

4 Fry the parsnip ribbons in the same pan used for the aubergine, topping up the vegetable oil if necessary, until golden and crisp. Lift out of the pan and transfer to a tray lined with kitchen paper. Season with salt and ground cumin.

5 Dress the rocket with the rest of the olive oil and the lemon juice. Spread a spoonful of whipped feta onto the base of each bun and top with the rocket followed by the aubergine slices, red pepper, beetroot, pickled cucumber and parsnip crisps. Spoon the mayonnaise onto the top bun and place on top.

7 SLOW-COOKED

BRAISED

PEARL BARLEY

With butternut, barberry & saffron aioli

Braising the barley in this recipe brings out its natural creaminess, much the same as cooking oats when making porridge, or similar to making risotto.

100ml (3½fl oz) water
100g (3½oz) caster sugar
30g (1oz) barberries
50ml (1¾fl oz) olive oil, plus
    extra to serve
2 small banana shallots,
    finely chopped
2 celery stalks, diced
1 garlic clove, grated
1 butternut squash, peeled
    and cut into 2.5cm (1in)
    dice
240g (8½oz) pearl barley
Zest of 1 orange, thinly
    julienned or sliced
1 litre (34fl oz) vegetable
    stock
1 tbsp coriander leaves,
    roughly chopped
1 tbsp finely chopped dill
    leaves
Juice of 1 lemon
4 tbsp Saffron Aioli (page
    193)
Flaked sea salt and ground
    black pepper
Extra-virgin olive oil,
    to serve

1 Combine the water and sugar in a small saucepan and bring to the boil over medium-high heat, stirring to dissolve the sugar. Reduce the heat and simmer for 3 minutes, then add the barberries and immediately remove from the heat. Allow the barberries to soak in the stock syrup for at least 10–15 minutes. These can be made ahead of time and will keep for up to 5 days.

2 Heat the olive oil in a large, heavy-based frying pan over medium heat and add the shallots and celery. Cook for 7–10 minutes, until soft and translucent but not coloured. Add the garlic and butternut squash, stir through to ensure everything is well coated and continue to fry for a few more minutes. Turn the heat up to medium-high, add the barley and orange zest, and cook until lightly toasted and aromatic. Slowly pour in just enough stock to just cover the grains and give everything a good stir. Bring to the boil, then lower the heat to a gentle simmer and cook for 30–35 minutes, or until the barley is tender but retains some bite. Top up the pan with 50ml (1¾fl oz) vegetable stock as and when needed to ensure the pan doesn't dry out, and stir regularly to prevent it catching underneath. By the time the barley is cooked most of the liquid should have been absorbed or reduced.

3 Just before serving, fold the herbs and lemon juice through and season to taste with salt and black pepper.

4 Divide the barley between serving plates and top with a generous spoonful of barberries, along with some of the syrup drizzled over the top for extra sweetness. Spoon a heaped tablespoon of saffron aioli onto each serving and finish with a generous glug of extra-virgin olive oil. Serve immediately.

TIP   Barberries are very small berries with a citrus-sharp flavour, which can be too intense if not soaked in sugar stock. You can find them in most Middle Eastern, Persian or Turkish grocery stores, but you could use sour cherries or dried cranberries instead, just skip the first step.

BUTTERBEANS

With samphire, poached egg & garlic-chilli oil

If you can't find any samphire, blanched asparagus would work well here. These butterbeans improve with time, so make enough to see you through the week.

CHILLI-GARLIC OIL
120ml (4fl oz) olive oil
4 garlic cloves, sliced
1½ tbsp dried chilli flakes

BUTTERBEANS
400g (14oz) dried
    butterbeans, covered
    with water by 5cm (2in)
    and soaked overnight
1 onion, cut in half
1 carrot, peeled and cut in
    half lengthways
1 bouquet garni
80ml (2½fl oz) olive oil
2 banana shallots, finely
    chopped
3 celery stalks, chopped
1 red pepper, deseeded
    and finely chopped
150ml (5fl oz) white wine
2 bay leaves
Few rosemary sprigs
½ courgette, thinly sliced
    to 2mm (1/16in) rounds
1 red chilli, finely diced
50ml (1¾fl oz) good-quality
    white wine vinegar
4 eggs
Grated zest of 1 lemon
120g (4½oz) samphire,
    blanched in boiling
    water then refreshed in
    iced water (optional)
Flaked sea salt and ground
    black pepper

FOR THE CHILLI-GARLIC OIL

1 Heat the oil in a heavy-based saucepan over medium heat until shimmering but not smoking. Add the garlic and chilli flakes to the pan, reduce the heat to medium-low and cook the garlic gently for 7–10 minutes, stirring regularly, until light golden brown and infused. Remove the garlic with a slotted spoon and transfer to a bowl lined with kitchen paper. Set the oil aside until needed.

FOR THE BUTTERBEANS

1 Drain the butterbeans and place in a deep saucepan covered with water by at least 5cm (2in). Add the onion, carrot and bouquet garni and bring to the boil over high heat. Reduce the heat to low and gently simmer for 45 minutes, or until the butterbeans are tender but not falling apart. Drain, remove the onion, carrot and bouquet garni and set aside, reserving the cooking liquor.

2 Heat the oil in a heavy-based saucepan over medium heat and gently cook the shallots, celery and red pepper for 5–7 minutes, until softened but not coloured. Season with salt and black pepper. Add the butterbeans to the pot and stir through, then add the wine. Turn up the heat to high and bring to a boil, then reduce the heat and simmer for 5–7 minutes, until the liquid has reduced by two-thirds. Pour 200ml (7fl oz) of the reserved bean cooking liquor back into the pan, as well the bay leaves, rosemary, courgette and chilli. Bring back to the boil then lower the heat and simmer for a further 10–15 minutes until reduced and slightly thickened.

3 Meanwhile, bring a small saucepan of water to the boil over high heat, add a splash of vinegar and reduce the heat to low. Gently crack your eggs into the pan and poach according to preference. I like my whites soft and the yolk still runny, 2½–3 minutes or thereabouts, depending on the size of egg used.

4 Remove the beans from the heat and check for seasoning. Fold through the vinegar and lemon zest, and transfer to serving bowls. Drench each serving liberally with the chilli and garlic oil and garnish with the blanched samphire, crisp garlic and poached egg on top. Serve immediately.

TAJINE OF SWEET POTATO, PUMPKIN & SWISS CHARD

There are few moments in life as gloriously revealing as lifting a tajine cone from its base to uncover the fragrant, stewed mass beneath.

The cooking time for this tajine will depend largely on how chunky you cut your veg. I like to leave mine on the large side as I think it looks more wholesome and provides interest in shape and texture. The longer cooking time also allows for the flavours to develop and intensify. By all means cut them slightly smaller if you're not blessed with an abundance of time but avoid dicing them too small. Nobody wants a homogeneous pile of vegetables that are disintegrating into the sauce.

3 large Swiss chard leaves, ribs removed, leaves shredded

60ml (2fl oz) olive oil

1 large white onion, thinly sliced

2 garlic cloves, crushed

¾ tsp ground cumin

¾ tsp ground coriander

½ tsp ground cinnamon

½ tsp ground ginger

400g (14oz) sweet potato, peeled and cut into 2.5cm (1in) chunks

400g (14oz) pumpkin, peeled and cut into 2.5cm (1in) chunks

200ml (7fl oz) water

2 bay leaves

400g (14oz) tin of chopped tomatoes

1 tbsp lemon juice

1 tsp caster sugar (optional)

5g (¼oz) coriander, roughly chopped

5g (¼oz) flat-leaf parsley, roughly chopped

1 tbsp harissa

Sea salt and black pepper

1 Place the Swiss chard in a heatproof bowl, cover with boiling water for 30 seconds, drain and refresh the chard in iced water. Squeeze dry and set aside until needed.

2 Heat 3 tablespoons of the olive oil over medium heat in a tajine or large heavy-based pan that has a lid and fry the onion, stirring occasionally, for 7–10 minutes until lightly coloured.

3 Add the garlic and spices, and fry for 2–3 minutes until fragrant. Add the sweet potato and pumpkin and fry for 5–7 minutes. Pour in the water, scraping any caramelized bits off the bottom of the tajine. Throw in the bay leaves and tomatoes, bring to the boil and lower the heat to a gentle simmer. Cover and cook for 40–50 minutes or until the vegetables are tender, and the sauce has reduced to a thickened gravy. Season to taste, then fold through the Swiss chard and lemon juice. Taste and add sugar to balance the acidity if needed.

4 Garnish the tajine with the chopped herbs. Mix the remaining olive oil with the harissa and drizzle over the top. Serve hot with a bowl of couscous, buttered rice or some warmed crusty bread.

AUBERGINE & RED PEPPER STEW

With cinnamon, walnuts & chickpeas

Here's a hearty stew with Persian roots. I've used chickpeas in this recipe, but butterbeans or cannellini would also work well.

2 large aubergines
Table salt
Vegetable oil, for frying
80ml (2½fl oz) extra-virgin
    olive oil
2 red onions, thinly sliced
2 red peppers, cut into
    2.5cm (1in) dice
3 garlic cloves, thinly
    sliced
150g (5½oz) tomato paste
1 tsp ground allspice
1 tsp ground cinnamon
800ml (27fl oz) water
400g (14oz) tin of
    chickpeas, drained
    and rinsed
50g (1¾oz) shelled
    walnuts, coarsely
    chopped (optional)
Small handful of coriander
    leaves
Buttered rice or grilled pita
    breads, to serve

❶ Cut the aubergines in half lengthways, then cut each half in half again and segment each quarter into three wedges. Sprinkle the wedges liberally with salt and set aside in a colander for 1–2 hours (this draws out the bitter juices). Rinse well under cold running water and pat dry with kitchen paper.

❷ Pour enough oil to come up the sides of a deep saucepan by 2–2.5cm (¾–1in) and set over medium heat until hot (roughly 180°C/350°F if you have a thermometer probe to hand).

❸ Shallow-fry the aubergine wedges in batches, making sure not to overcrowd the pan, turning on both sides and frying for 5–7 minutes or until golden brown but still holding shape. Remove the aubergines from the oil using a slotted spoon, then drain on kitchen paper and set aside.

❹ Heat the olive oil in a heavy-based saucepan over medium-high heat until shimmering hot, then add the onions to the pan to sear, stirring regularly for 7–10 minutes, until softened and caramelized at the edges.

❺ Add the red peppers and garlic, and continue to fry for 5 minutes, stirring regularly until softened. Add the tomato paste, allspice and cinnamon, and stir to combine. Pour in the water, then add the aubergine and very gently toss so as to mix everything through without breaking up the pieces. Add the chickpeas to the pan, turn the heat to high and bring to the boil. Reduce the heat to low and gently simmer for 20–25 minutes, until thickened and reduced.

❻ Transfer to a serving bowl, garnish with chopped walnuts (if using) and picked coriander leaves. Serve with rice or grilled pita bread.

STEWED WHITE BEANS (LOUBIA)

With cumin & coriander

These stewed beans, from the streets of Morocco, are heavily spiced and very fragrant. A warm, soothing hug in a bowl and a go-to order of mine at almost every Moroccan eatery I stop at along my travels. The key to this dish is in the sauce, which needs to be reduced to a thickened gravy, but still saucy enough to allow for mopping action.

2 tbsp olive oil
1 small onion, chopped
3 garlic cloves, grated
1 tsp cumin seeds
1½ tbsp tomato paste
1 tsp harissa (optional)
3 tomatoes, grated
½ tsp ground cumin
1½ tsp sweet paprika
1 tsp ground turmeric
½ tsp ground ginger
250g (9oz) dried white beans (haricot or cannellini), soaked in water overnight and drained
10g (1/3oz) flat-leaf parsley, chopped
10g (1/3oz) coriander, chopped
1 litre (34fl oz) water
1 tbsp lemon juice
1 tsp sugar
1 preserved lemon, pulp removed, rind finely sliced (optional)
1 lemon, quartered
Flaked sea salt and coarse black pepper
Olive oil, to serve

1 Heat the oil in a heavy-based, deep saucepan over medium heat and sweat the onion for 7–10 minutes, until softened and translucent. Add the garlic and cumin seeds and fry for 2–3 minutes to infuse and soften, then add the tomato paste and, if using, the harissa. Stir, cooking the paste out for 2–3 minutes, then add the grated tomatoes and spices. Add the drained beans, parsley, half the coriander and pour in the water.

2 Bring to the boil over high heat, then reduce to a gentle simmer, cover and cook for 1½–2 hours or until the beans are completely tender and almost falling apart (depending on your beans, this can take up to 4 hours). You want to ensure the beans are completely softened, and the sauce is reduced to a thickened gravy. Throughout cooking, top up with a little bit more water or cover the pan with a tight-fitting lid as and when needed, to slow the speed at which the sauce reduces, or remove the lid and let the sauce bubble away until reduced.

3 Once satisfied with how the beans are cooked and the consistency of the sauce, remove the pan from the heat, season with salt, black pepper, lemon juice and sugar; taste for balance. Ladle the beans into serving bowls and serve piping hot, with a final generous drizzle of extra-virgin olive oil, the rest of the coriander on top, some preserved lemon rind (if using) and a lemon wedge for optional squeezing, along with some crusty bread of course.

FUL MEDAMES

Ful medames, a sort of mashed paste made of dried broad (fava) beans, is not one for the eye admittedly, but what it lacks in looks it more than makes up for in unadulterated deliciousness. You want to cook the beans on a slow simmer, for what feels like an inordinate amount of time (you may need 4–6 hours of cooking time). They should practically disintegrate into a coarse paste, with only some gentle persuasion by way of a firm stir or a crushing with the back of a fork. You may prefer the beans to be slightly firmer, to still hold their shape, which is fine too – just pull them off slightly earlier when you're happy with their consistency.

300g (10½oz) dried fava
  beans
1 tbsp ground cumin
2 lemons, 1 juiced,
  1 quartered
2 garlic cloves, grated
2 hot green chillies, very
  finely chopped
3 tomatoes, chopped
½ red onion, finely
  chopped
90ml (3fl oz) extra-virgin
  olive oil
2 tbsp chopped coriander
25g (1oz) crème fraîche
  (optional)
Flaked sea salt and coarse
  black pepper
Pita breads or flatbreads,
  to serve

1 Soak the fava beans in a large pan overnight with at least four times the volume of water.

2 Place the pan over high heat and bring to the boil, then lower the heat to a gentle simmer and cook the beans for 4–6 hours until meltingly soft and tender, skimming away the foam from the surface as needed. Top the pan up with water if it runs too low – make sure not to let the pan dry out otherwise the beans will catch and burn on the bottom of the pan. The fava beans can take a long time to cook through, sometimes even overnight, so be patient with them and resist the urge to pull them off too soon.

3 Once the beans are tender to the point of completely falling apart, season with salt and black pepper and stir through the cumin. Mash the beans with a potato masher or the back of a fork so that they are crushed slightly but remain chunky and coarse for texture and appearance. Place on a very low heat or cover and transfer to a low oven to keep warm while you prepare the toppings.

4 Combine the lemon juice, garlic and green chillies in a small bowl and set aside to macerate for 10–15 minutes. Dress the tomatoes and red onion with 2 tablespoons olive oil, and season.

5 Spoon the beans onto serving plates and dress with the macerated green chillies, the remaining olive oil and the tomato salsa. Garnish with chopped coriander, an entirely optional dollop of crème fraîche and a lemon quarter. Serve immediately with freshly grilled pita or flatbread.

BRAISED
CANNELLINI BEANS

These beans are delicious on their own with nothing more than some crusty bread to mop them all up.

250g (9oz) dried cannellini beans
2 rosemary sprigs
2 thyme sprigs
3 garlic cloves, smashed
1 bay leaf
2 carrots, 1 halved lengthways, 1 finely chopped
2 onions, 1 halved, 1 finely chopped
1 large sweet potato
120ml (4fl oz) olive oil
1 celery stalk, chopped
1 red pepper, deseeded and finely diced
2 garlic cloves, sliced
2 tbsp best-quality red wine vinegar
30g (1oz) flat-leaf parsley, finely chopped
80g (2¾oz) crème fraîche
60g (2oz) Crispy Shallots (page 200 or store-bought), optional
40g (1½oz) Confit Chilli Ezme (page 195), optional
2 Preserved Lemons (page 202 or shop-bought), rind only, finely sliced (optional)
80g (2¾oz) Pickled Fennel and Orange (page 201), optional
Flaked sea salt and ground black pepper

1 Place the dried cannellini beans in a bowl covered with water by 5cm (2in) and leave to soak overnight.

2 Preheat the oven to 200°C/400°F/180°C Fan/Gas Mark 6. Drain the beans and transfer to a heavy-based saucepan. Cover with water and bring to the boil over high heat. Reduce to a simmer, add the rosemary, thyme, garlic, bay leaf, halved carrot and halved onion, then stir through and cook the beans for 1–1½ hours or until tender but not falling apart. Top up the pan with water if it gets too low.

3 Meanwhile, pierce the sweet potato several times with a fork and roast in the oven for 1–1½ hours or until completely tender. Set aside.

4 When the beans are cooked, drain but reserve about 100ml (3½fl oz) of the cooking liquor. Spread the beans out on a tray to cool and remove all of the aromatics when cool enough to do so.

5 Heat 3 tablespoons olive oil in a heavy-based frying pan until shimmering, add the chopped onion and carrot, celery and red pepper and cook for 7–10 minutes until softened and translucent. Add the garlic and fry for 2–3 minutes, followed by the drained beans. Cook briefly for a few minutes to bring the flavours together, then ladle the reserved stock into the pan and cook over medium-high heat for a few minutes or until the stock has reduced by about two-thirds and the beans have warmed through.

6 Remove the pan from the heat, fold the vinegar and flat-leaf parsley through, followed by the rest of the olive oil. Season to taste with salt and pepper. Transfer to a serving plate, remove the flesh from the sweet potato, discarding the skin. Place on top of the beans and garnish with a large dollop of crème fraîche and, if using, the crispy shallots, confit chilli ezme, preserved lemon and pickled fennel and orange.

ROMANO BEANS

With tahina & egg

Loubieh Bi Zeit is a Lebanese dish of beans braised in olive oil, tomato sauce and plenty of garlic, served warm or at room temperature as a mezze. This is a variation on a theme, using Romano beans instead of green beans, but you can swap them out if you prefer.

2 tbsp olive oil
½ onion, finely chopped
3 garlic cloves, sliced
1 tsp cumin seeds, toasted
    and ground
1 tsp coriander seeds,
    toasted and ground
1 tsp Persian dried black
    lime, grated or ground
    (optional)
1 tbsp tomato paste
200g (7oz) passata
200ml (7fl oz) vegetable
    stock
80g (2¾oz) cherry
    tomatoes
400g (14oz) Romano
    beans
1 tsp lemon thyme leaves
1 tbsp pomegranate
    molasses
Juice of ½ lemon
Picked dill leaves
60g (2oz) Basic Tahina
    Sauce (page 199)
2 hard-boiled eggs, peeled
    and sliced
Extra-virgin olive oil, to
    serve
Flaked sea salt and ground
    black pepper

❶ Heat the oil in a heavy-based, deep saucepan over medium heat. Add the onion and garlic and cook for 7–10 minutes, until softened and translucent but not coloured. Add the ground seeds and Persian lime (if using) and cook for 2–3 minutes, until fragrant.

❷ Stir through the tomato paste and allow it to infuse in the oil for a few minutes, then pour in the passata and vegetable stock. Bring to a simmer, throw in the cherry tomatoes, beans and picked lemon thyme leaves, return to a gentle simmer and reduce the heat to low. Continue to cook for 15–20 minutes until the beans have softened completely.

❸ Season liberally with salt and a few grinds of black pepper to taste, fold through the pomegranate molasses and lemon juice, and transfer to a serving plate. Scatter the dill leaves over the beans and finish with a generous dollop of tahina sauce and the sliced eggs. A final glug of olive oil over the top wouldn't go amiss either.

TIP   The tahina sauce and boiled egg make welcome additions but aren't essential. Serve this dish with plain rice, warm pita bread or some crusty baguette – whatever takes your fancy.

RISOTTO OF FREEKEH

With confit garlic & sourdough breadcrumbs

Risotto has always been one of my favourite dishes to prepare. I enjoy the ritualistic process of ladling in the stock gradually, diligently waiting for it to be absorbed before adding more. It is a dish of love and should be tended to with care and attention and never left to its own devices. Freekeh is similar to bulgur, and is made from green durum wheat that has been roasted and cracked to create its unique flavour, which is nutty with a satisfying earthiness to it.

150g (5½oz) freekeh
25ml (¾fl oz) olive oil
25g (1oz) unsalted butter
2 small banana shallots, finely chopped
2 celery stalks, chopped
2 garlic cloves, minced
1½ tbsp tomato paste
150ml (5fl oz) dry white wine
320ml (11fl oz) vegetable stock
½ tsp smoked paprika
50g (1¾oz) sun-dried tomatoes, chopped
50g (1¾oz) black olives, pitted and chopped
1 level tsp chopped thyme
2 tbsp Crispy Sourdough Breadcrumbs (page 188)
50g (1¾oz) Confit Garlic (page 193)
60g (2oz) Confit Chilli Ezme (page 195), optional
Small handful of flat-leaf parsley leaves
Flaked sea salt and ground black pepper
Extra-virgin olive oil

1 Soak the freekeh in cold water for 5–10 minutes, or until the water runs clear when washed under a running tap.

2 Heat the oil and butter in a large heavy-based pan over medium heat and add the shallots and celery. Cook for 7–10 minutes, until soft and translucent but not coloured. Add the garlic and stir through for a few minutes, then add the tomato paste and continue to cook for a further 2–3 minutes, stirring regularly.

3 Add the freekeh to the pan and stir until coated. Throw in the wine and reduce until almost all of it has been absorbed. Pour in the stock, ladle by ladle, and simmer for 25–30 minutes until fully absorbed by the freekeh, then season with salt and black pepper and stir well. Fold through the smoked paprika, sun-dried tomatoes, olives and thyme, and remove from the heat.

4 Spoon the risotto onto serving dishes, sprinkle the sourdough crumb over the top, stud each plate with confit garlic and top with an optional dollop of confit chilli ezme. Garnish with picked flat-leaf parsley leaves and a final drizzle of your best olive oil.

8 PURÉED

CHOPPED

Serves 4 as a
light meal or 6
as a mezze

HUMMUS

Wild mushrooms, egg yolk & tarragon

Egg yolk on hummus is not one for the purists, and there are a few countries across the Middle East that I probably won't be allowed back into having published this recipe, but I think it works well here, especially with the luxurious wild mushrooms, another component which might raise eyebrows among hummus devotees.

HUMMUS

280g (10oz) dried
    chickpeas
½ tsp bicarbonate of soda
1 onion, peeled and halved
6 garlic cloves, 4 peeled
    and left whole, 2 finely
    chopped or grated
½ tbsp salt
200g (7oz) tahini paste
40ml (1¼fl oz) lemon juice
1 tsp ground cumin
2–3 tbsp Basic Tahina
    Sauce (page 199)
1 egg yolk
2 tbsp olive oil
Few tarragon leaves

WILD MUSHROOMS

60ml (2fl oz) olive oil
250g (9oz) shiitake
    mushrooms, cleaned
    and quartered
100g (3½oz) chanterelle
    mushrooms, cleaned
1 garlic clove, finely grated
2 tbsp lemon juice
Flaked sea salt and ground
    black pepper

FOR THE HUMMUS

1 Soak the chickpeas in a large pan overnight with the bicarbonate of soda and four times the volume of water.

2 Place over high heat and bring to the boil, then remove the chickpeas, drain and rinse well. Return the chickpeas to the pan, add the onion and whole garlic cloves, refill with water and bring back to the boil, then lower the heat and gently simmer for 2–4 hours until meltingly soft and tender. Skim the surface of foam throughout cooking and top the pan up with water if it runs low to prevent the chickpeas from catching on the bottom of the pan.

3 Once the chickpeas are tender and almost completely falling apart, turn off the heat, season with the salt and set aside for 30 minutes or so. Strain the chickpeas and reserve the cooking liquor. Pick out the garlic and onion. Transfer the chickpeas to a food processor, add the tahini paste, lemon juice, cumin and grated garlic, and blitz, gradually pouring in the reserved cooking liquor until you have a smooth and creamy texture. Taste for seasoning.

4 Transfer the hummus to a serving plate and spread around its parameter using the back of a spoon. Spoon the tahini sauce in a puddle in the middle and top with the wild mushrooms. Make a well in the middle for the egg yolk, drizzle with the olive oil and finish with a few tarragon leaves.

FOR THE WILD MUSHROOMS

1 Heat a large frying pan over high heat. Add the olive oil and, when hot, add the shiitake mushrooms. Don't overcrowd the pan; it's important they sear and don't steam. Cook, without stirring, for 3 minutes until the mushrooms are well browned. Add the chanterelle mushrooms and fry for a further 1–2 minutes. Add the garlic and give the mushrooms a good toss to turn them for a minute being careful not to let the garlic burn or colour. Add the lemon juice, scraping any sticky bits from the base of the pan, season generously with salt and black pepper to taste, and remove from the heat.

PUMPKIN CHERSHI

With Aleppo chilli butter

Chershi (or tershi) is a spicy Libyan spread made with pumpkin and lots of garlic. It's a great starter, as part of a spread of dips or mezze, that will invariably have your guests fighting over who gets the last scraps. You can make a half recipe if you'd prefer, or keep some back in the fridge for another time.

The caraway seeds lend a fragrant bittersweet sharpness that comes together with the pumpkin and harissa perfectly. The Aleppo chilli butter adds a decadent and rich finish, but you can omit this in favour of a good-quality olive oil.

2 tbsp olive oil

1 red onion, roughly chopped

1 tsp ground cumin

½ tsp caraway seeds, toasted

¾ tsp ground coriander

6 garlic cloves, sliced

1½ tbsp tomato paste

30g (1oz) harissa

600g (1lb 5oz) pumpkin, peeled and cut into 2.5cm (1in) chunks

1½ tbsp sugar

1 tbsp lemon juice

2 tbsp Aleppo Chilli Butter (page 160)

5g (¼oz) picked dill, roughly chopped

2 tsp each black and white sesame seeds, toasted

Flaked sea salt and ground black pepper

Pita breads or flatbreads, lightly brushed with oil and warmed in the oven or grill, to serve

1 Warm the olive oil in a wide, heavy-based saucepan over medium heat and cook the onion, stirring regularly, for 5–7 minutes or until softened and translucent. Add the cumin, caraway seeds, ground coriander and garlic, and fry for 2 minutes. Stir in the tomato paste and harissa, and cook out for 2–3 minutes. Add a couple tablespoons of water, scraping off any of the flavoursome bits that may have become stuck to the base of the pan to deglaze, then add the pumpkin chunks, sugar and 100ml (3½fl oz) water. Reduce the heat to a low and gently simmer, covered, for 15–18 minutes, until the pumpkin is just tender.

2 Transfer the pumpkin to a blender and pulse to a coarse purée or dip. In the absence of a blender, or alternatively, you can mash the pumpkin with the back of a fork – it will yield a chunkier texture, but this may be preferable. Tast for seasoning and adjust accordingly with salt and black pepper, then fold through the lemon juice.

3 Transfer the chershi to a serving plate, drizzle with Aleppo chilli butter and garnish with the dill and the toasted sesame seeds. Serve at room temperature with grilled pita or flatbreads.

WATERMELON GAZPACHO

With avocado

Gazpacho, to my mind at least, is intended for improvisation. There are no hard-and-fast rules as to what ingredients should go into one. I marinate my gazpacho ingredients before processing them in the blender as this gives the ingredients a chance to mingle. If you're short of time, you can skip this. With that said, gazpacho always tastes better the day after it's been made, as the flavours become more complex. Chill your gazpacho before serving as it needs to hit your guests fridge-cold for maximum impact.

500g (1lb 2oz) watermelon, rind removed, chopped into large chunks
600g (1lb 5oz) plum tomatoes, cored and diced
½ red onion, chopped
1 cucumber, ½ peeled, deseeded and chopped, ½ diced
150g (5½oz) red peppers, deseeded and chopped
1 red chilli, sliced
3 garlic cloves, chopped
5g (¼oz) mint, chopped
10g (⅓oz) basil
120g (4½oz) best-quality white bread, crusts removed and cut into chunks
50ml (1¾fl oz) sherry vinegar
150ml (5fl oz) extra-virgin olive oil, plus extra to serve
1 ripe avocado
2 spring onions, sliced
1 tbsp lemon juice
Flaked sea salt and ground black pepper

1 Combine the watermelon, tomatoes, red onion, the peeled cucumber, peppers, chilli, garlic, mint, half the basil and the bread in a large bowl. Stir and set aside in the fridge for 2–4 hours to marinate.

2 Transfer the ingredients from the bowl to a food processor and blend until smooth. Pour in the sherry vinegar and 120ml (4fl oz) olive oil and pulse to combine. Season with salt and black pepper to taste. Set aside in the fridge to chill until needed.

3 Peel and destone the avocado, then dice it and combine in a small bowl with the spring onions, diced cucumber and remaining olive oil, and lemon juice. Season to taste with salt.

4 Transfer the gazpacho to individual serving bowls, top each bowl with avocado salsa and garnish with the reserved basil, torn into pieces. Finish with a final drizzle of olive oil and serve.

BYSSARA

With paprika oil

Byssara, a thick, sludge-like soup that tastes far better than it looks, is the national dish of Egypt. I've only had it in Morocco, sold by hawkers down the cobbled back streets of Marrakech's medina, as well as road-side eateries up and down the country.

It's often served for breakfast and one of my most memorable travel experiences was sitting down to a bowl on a tiny makeshift stool, surrounded by Moroccans from all walks of life on their way to work, all staring intensely at me with bewildered amusement that I was joining their daily custom.

400g (9oz) dried
fava beans
4 garlic cloves, peeled
100ml (3½fl oz) lemon juice
150ml (5fl oz) best-quality
extra- virgin olive oil
1½ tsp dried chilli flakes
2 tsp cumin seeds, toasted
1 tsp sweet paprika
1 green chilli, finely
chopped
2 tbsp chopped coriander
1 tbsp coarse sea salt
mixed with 1 tbsp
ground cumin, to serve

❶ Place the fava beans in a large pan with at least four times the volume of water. Allow to soak overnight.

❷ The next day, place the pan over high heat, add the garlic and bring to the boil, then lower the heat and gently simmer for 4–6 hours, or until meltingly soft and tender. Skim the surface of foam throughout cooking and top the pan up with water if it runs low to prevent the beans from catching on the bottom of the pan.

❸ Drain the beans, reserving any cooking liquor that is left, and transfer to a food processor. Add the lemon juice, 100ml (3½fl oz) olive oil, 1 tsp chilli flakes and the cumin seeds, and blend until smooth. Check for consistency, pouring in the reserved cooking liquor (or extra warm water) to thin out the soup as desired. The soup should be moderately thick, almost sludge-like but definitely still pourable. Taste for seasoning and adjust accordingly with salt, black pepper and more lemon juice.

❹ Warm the rest of the oil in a small pan over medium-high heat until sizzling, and add the paprika and reserved chilli flakes, swirling the pan until the oil turns red, then remove immediately from the heat.

❺ Serve the soup piping hot, drizzled with the paprika oil and garnished with chopped green chilli, coriander and cumin salt.

SPINACH BORANI

With fried chickpeas

Borani is a dish of Persian origin, though there are Turkish variations, usually involving yoghurt as a base or topping. It comes in all different shapes and forms depending on where you are in the world, some with meat, and many using blanched or sautéed vegetables that are subsequently blended or incorporated into the yoghurt.

Fried chickpeas are a great topping for many dips and spreads, such as Pumpkin Chershi (page 148). At our Shawarma Bar, we garnish our hummus with fried chickpeas. If you'd rather not go to the effort of making them, this borani will taste delicious all by itself.

Sunflower oil, for
    deep-frying
100g (3½oz) drained tinned
    chickpeas, rinsed and
    patted dry
½ tbsp za'atar
¼ tsp ground turmeric
200g (7oz) spinach
200g (7oz) natural yoghurt
2 garlic cloves, minced
1½ tbsp lemon juice
50ml (2fl oz) extra-virgin
    olive oil
1 tbsp dill
Flaked sea salt and ground
    black pepper
Pita breads or flatbreads,
    lightly brushed with
    oil and warmed in the
    oven or grill, to serve

1 Pour sunflower oil into a heavy-based saucepan to a 2cm (¾in) depth. Place the pan over medium-high heat until the oil is 200°C (400°F) when probed with a thermometer. Lower the chickpeas into the hot oil to deep-fry for 8-10 minutes, or until golden brown and crisp. Remove the chickpeas from the oil with a slotted spoon, transfer to a plate lined with kitchen paper, sprinkle with the za'atar and turmeric, and season generously with salt and black pepper.

2 Bring a saucepan of salted water to the boil and blanch the spinach for 30 seconds, drain and refresh in a bowl filled with iced water, or under cold running water. Drain and squeeze dry with your hands to remove as much of the liquid as possible. Finely chop the spinach and add to a bowl. Stir through the yoghurt, garlic and lemon juice. Fold in half the olive oil. Season to taste with salt and black pepper.

3 Spread the borani around the base of a plate and spoon over the deep-fried chickpeas. Garnish with chopped dill and finish with a generous drizzle of the remaining olive oil around the outside. Serve with warmed bread.

BURNT AUBERGINE SOUP

With rice & herbs

This recipe was born out of needing to use up some aubergines that were about to go bad. It's one of those 'grab what you can find' concoctions that ends up working out far better than you first thought possible. It's now a firm favourite in my household. I threw the rice in to lure my four-year-old daughter to the party and it worked a treat. The chilli was a later addition that can be omitted if you're cooking for kids but adds a lovely warming and gentle heat that complements the aubergine perfectly.

3 medium aubergines
90ml (3fl oz) olive oil
1 large onion, chopped
1 tbsp cumin seeds
3 garlic cloves, minced
1 red chilli, sliced
3 large tomatoes, diced
800ml (27fl oz) vegetable
   stock
½ tbsp lemon juice
1 tbsp sugar
120g (4½oz) long-grain
   rice, rinsed several
   times under running
   water and drained
10g (¹/₃oz) dill, finely
   chopped
10g (¹/₃oz) flat-leaf parsley,
   chopped
40g (1½oz) crème fraîche
2 tbsp grated lemon zest
2 tbsp Crispy Shallots
   (page 200), optional
Flaked sea salt and ground
   black pepper
Best-quality extra-virgin
   olive oil, to serve

1 Set a barbecue up for direct grilling. In the absence of a barbecue you can also use the open flame from the hob. (It's a good idea to line the stovetop with foil to avoid excess mess.)

2 Pierce the aubergines several times with a fork and place over the coals or directly over the flame on your stovetop. Char the aubergines all over, turning regularly, until blackened and soft. Remove once cooked all the way through and set aside until they are cool enough to handle.

3 When cool enough to handle, peel the aubergines and chop the aubergine flesh into large chunks. Transfer to a bowl or tray, drizzle with 60ml (2fl oz) olive oil and season generously with salt and black pepper. Allow the aubergines to sit while you get on with making the soup.

4 Add the remaining olive oil to a large pan and set over a medium heat. Add the onion and cumin seeds and cook, stirring regularly, for 5–7 minutes or until softened. Add the garlic and chilli, then continue to fry for 2–3 minutes. Stir in the tomatoes then add the stock, lemon juice, sugar and drained rice. Turn the heat down to low and gently simmer for 20–25 minutes, until the rice is just tender and the soup flavourful. About 5 minutes before the end of cooking, add the aubergines to the soup just to warm through. Taste for seasoning and adjust accordingly.

5 Ladle the soup into serving bowls, garnish with the herbs, a dollop of crème fraîche, lemon zest and, if using, crispy shallots. Finish with a generous glug of extra-virgin olive oil and serve piping hot.

BABA GHANOUSH

With dried cranberries & hazelnuts

I particularly like the way the nuttiness of chopped hazelnuts and tahini pair with the sweetness of dried cranberries (though you could also use apricots or sour cherries too). Together they provide a lovely textural and flavour contrast to the soft mass of aubergine flesh. We play around with our toppings for baba ghanoush. The combinations are virtually endless, aubergine having a chameleon-like ability to adapt to its surroundings.

3 medium aubergines
3 garlic cloves, grated
Grated zest and juice of
    1 lemon
2 tbsp tahini paste
70ml (2¼fl oz) olive oil, plus
    extra to drizzle
1½ tbsp chopped flat-leaf
    parsley
1½ tbsp chopped
    coriander
1 tbsp dried cranberries
20g (¾oz) hazelnuts,
    toasted and roughly
    chopped
Flaked sea salt and ground
    black pepper
Pita breads or flatbreads,
    lightly brushed with
    oil and warmed in the
    oven or on the grill,
    to serve

1 Set a barbecue up for direct grilling. In the absence of a barbecue you can also use the open flame from the hob. (It's a good idea to line the stovetop with foil to avoid excess mess.)

2 Pierce the aubergines several times with a fork and place over the coals or directly over the flame on your stovetop. Char the aubergines all over, turning regularly, until blackened and soft. Remove once cooked all the way through and set aside until they are cool enough to handle.

3 When the aubergines are cool enough to handle, open each in half lengthways through the stem. Scoop out the flesh and chop until a coarse and chunky purée has formed. Add the garlic to the aubergine flesh and mix through.

4 Transfer the aubergine mix to a large bowl and add the lemon zest, juice, tahini, olive oil and half the herbs, and stir thoroughly to combine. Season with salt and black pepper to taste, adding more lemon juice if required.

5 Spoon the aubergine onto a serving plate, spreading it out slightly with the back of a spoon and garnish with dried cranberries, hazelnuts, the remaining herbs and a final drizzle of olive oil. Serve with warmed pita or flatbreads.

9 POACHED

STEAMED

SWEET POTATO & RICOTTA GNOCCHI

This is an old recipe that first appeared at Made In Camden, where I scored my first Head Chef position. My sous chef at the time, Eran Tibi, who now runs his own brilliant restaurant Bala Baya in Southwark, conceived of this dish. You can make the gnocchi in advance and store them in the fridge for 2–3 days or they can be cooked from frozen.

SWEET POTATO GNOCCHI

500g (1lb 2oz) sweet potato
200g (7oz) plain flour
220g (8oz) ricotta
50g (1¾oz) parmesan, grated
Pinch of grated nutmeg
1 egg, beaten
1½ tsp salt

BURNT AUBERGINE

2 aubergines
2 garlic cloves, grated or minced
Grated zest of 1 lemon and 1½ tbsp juice
2 tbsp best-quality extra-virgin olive oil
Flaked sea salt and ground black pepper

ALEPPO CHILLI BUTTER

80g (2¾oz) unsalted butter
1 tbsp Aleppo chilli flakes (pul biber)

FOR THE SWEET POTATO GNOCCHI

1 Preheat the oven to 200°C (400°F)/180°C Fan/Gas Mark 6. Pierce the sweet potato several times with a fork and roast in the oven for 40–50 minutes, until completely tender. Set aside until just cool enough to handle.

2 Dust 90g (3oz) of the flour onto a work surface and crumble the ricotta over it. Scoop the flesh of the sweet potato over the top and discard the skin. Add the grated parmesan, nutmeg, the beaten egg and salt, and mash with the back o' fork, gradually adding in the rest of the flour, bit by bit, until it all comes together in one craggy mess. If the dough is too wet, add a little more flour.

3 Set the dough aside, wrapped in clingfilm, for 20 minutes or so, cleaning your work surface in the interim. Dust the work surface with some more flour and roll the dough out to 2.5cm (1in) thickness. Cut the dough into strips about 2cm (¾in) in diameter and roll into a long sausage shape. Cut each strip into 2.5cm (1in) pieces using a knife and then use the back of fork to lightly press into the dough to imprint ridges on each piece. Transfer to a baking sheet, dust with more flour and set aside until needed.

FOR THE BURNT AUBERGINE

1 Set a barbecue up for direct grilling. In the absence of a barbecue you can also use the flame from the hob. (It's a good idea to line the stovetop with foil to avoid excess mess.) Pierce the aubergines several times with a fork and place over the coals or directly over the flame on your stove. Char the aubergines all over, turning regularly, until blackened and soft. Remove once cooked all the way through and set aside until its cool enough to handle.

2 Cut the aubergines open in half lengthways through the stem. Scoop out the flesh and chop until a coarse and chunky purée has formed. Add the garlic to the aubergine flesh and mix through. Transfer the aubergine mix to a large bowl and add the lemon zest, juice and olive oil, and stir thoroughly to combine. Season with flaked salt and black pepper to taste.

TO FINISH
50ml (1¾fl oz) olive oil
200g (7oz) spinach
100g (3½oz) Greek yoghurt
2 tbsp pine nuts, toasted
Few flat-leaf parsley leaves

FOR THE ALEPPO CHILLI BUTTER

1 Melt the butter over medium-low heat in a small saucepan. Whisk the butter gently as it cooks for 3–5 minutes, until darkened and caramelized to a nutty golden brown. Add the Aleppo chilli flakes right at the end, swirl the pan, then immediately remove the pan from the heat. Keep warm until ready to use.

TO FINISH

1 Bring a large, deep pan of salted water to the boil over high heat, reduce to a rolling simmer and tip the gnocchi into the pan. Cook for 1–2 minutes, until risen to the surface, then remove with a slotted spoon and transfer to a tray lined with kitchen paper. This step can also be prepared ahead of time.

2 Warm the oil in a heavy-based pan over medium-high heat, then add the gnocchi to the pan, tossing regularly, until well coloured and warmed through, about 4–5 minutes. Fold the spinach through for the final minute of cooking, just until wilted, then season. Spoon the aubergine on the base of a plate and lay the gnocchi and spinach on top. Dot over the yoghurt and drizzle with the Aleppo chilli butter. Sprinkle over the pine nuts and parsley. Serve piping hot.

MEJADERAH

With barberry, cardamom & pistachio

Mejaderah, a dish of lentils, rice, sweet spices and caramelized onion, is pimped up in this recipe with the addition of nuts and barberries. This is great as a side dish to accompany hearty stews such as Tajine of Sweet Potato, Pumpkin and Swiss Chard (page 133), but I also serve it as the main event too, accompanied by some hummus or tahina and fresh chopped salad.

50g (1¾oz) caster sugar
50ml (1¾fl oz) water
30g (1oz) barberries
2 tbsp olive oil
25g (1oz) unsalted butter
1 tbsp cardamom pods
2 cinnamon sticks, broken
    in half
1 tbsp cumin seeds
2 onions, thinly sliced
400g (14oz) basmati rice,
    washed
200g (7oz) cooked brown
    lentils
1 tsp ground allspice
1 tsp flaked sea salt
700ml (23½fl oz) boiling
    water
20g (¾oz) soft herbs
    (any combination of
    coriander, dill, flat-leaf
    parsley), chopped
80g (2¾oz) pistachios,
    toasted and roughly
    chopped
60g (2oz) flaked almonds,
    toasted
Coarse black pepper

1 Dissolve the sugar in the water in a small saucepan over high heat. Add the barberries then remove the pan from the heat immediately. Leave to soak in the syrup for at least 15 minutes. Drain and set aside until needed.

2 Heat the olive oil and butter in a heavy-based pan that has a lid over medium heat, add the cardamom pods, cinnamon sticks and cumin seeds, and fry for a few minutes until fragrant. Next, add the onions and cook, stirring occasionally, for 15–20 minutes or until softened and deep golden brown.

3 Add the rice to the onions and fry for 2–3 minutes, followed by the lentils, allspice, drained barberries, salt and several grinds of black pepper. Stir well, add the boiling water and cover with the lid. Reduce the heat to the lowest heat and cook the rice very gently for 20 minutes. Turn off the heat, quickly take off the lid, place a clean tea towel over the pan and replace the lid, allowing the rice to rest for 10 minutes or so. Add most of the chopped herbs (reserving some for garnish) and fork through the rice. Check for seasoning and adjust according to taste. Garnish with the chopped pistachios and almonds, plus the remaining herbs thrown over the top.

TIP — Barberries are easily found these days but if you can't find them, substitute with currants or sultanas.

EGYPTIAN KOSHARI

Koshari is a street food and national icon of Egypt, involving macaroni, lentils, rice, a rich tomato sauce, crunchy fried onions and a punchy garlic dressing.

GARLIC VINAIGRETTE

120g (4½oz) butter
50g (1¾oz) garlic (about 20 cloves), minced or crushed
Juice of 3 lemons
Flaked sea salt

TOMATO SAUCE

60ml (2fl oz) olive oil
4 garlic cloves, sliced
400g (14oz) tinned tomatoes, blitzed, or tomato passata
80g (2¾oz) Tomato-Chilli Jam (page 189)
150ml (5fl oz) water
1½ tsp dried chilli flakes
200g (7oz) tinned chickpeas, drained and rinsed

KOSHARI

Vegetable oil, for shallow-frying
60g (2oz) plain flour
1 small onion, finely sliced
180g (6½oz) dried brown lentils
2 tsp salt
150g (5½oz) basmati rice
225ml (7½fl oz) water
25g (1oz) unsalted butter
120g (4½oz) macaroni
2 tbsp finely chopped flat-leaf parsley

FOR THE GARLIC VINAIGRETTE

1 Melt the butter in small saucepan over medium heat. Add the garlic and fry for 2–3 minutes, skimming the surface to remove any foam, until golden brown. Remove the pan immediately from the heat to prevent the butter burning, season with salt and add the lemon juice, whisking to combine. Set aside.

FOR THE TOMATO SAUCE

1 Heat the olive oil in a heavy-based pan over medium heat and fry the garlic for 3–5 minutes until golden and softened but not burnt. Added the tinned tomatoes, tomato-chilli jam and water, and bring to a gentle simmer. Add the chilli flakes, turn the heat down to its lowest setting, and simmer gently for 25–30 minutes, until reduced and thickened. About 10 minutes before the end of the cooking time, add the chickpeas to the pan and stir through to combine. Season to taste with salt and set aside, kept warm, until needed. The sauce can be made ahead of time and reheated just prior to serving.

FOR THE KOSHARI

1 Pour enough oil to come up the sides of a deep saucepan by 1cm (½in) and set over medium heat until hot (roughly 180°C/350°F). Season the flour with salt and pepper. Dredge the onion in the flour, shaking off any excess. Fry in the hot oil, stirring frequently for 3–5 minutes, until golden brown, remove with a slotted spoon and drain on kitchen paper. Taste and adjust the seasoning.

2 Put the lentils in a large lidded pan, cover with water, add 1 teaspoon salt and bring to the boil over medium-high heat. Cover with a lid and cook the lentils for 20–25 minutes, or until softened to tender but not yet falling apart.

3 Rinse the rice in water, swirling several times to wash the starch from it. Drain and repeat at least twice, or until the water is clear. Transfer to a medium heavy-based saucepan with a tight-fitting lid and pour in the water, remaining 1 teaspoon salt and the butter. Bring to the boil and cook, with the lid on, for 12–15 minutes or until the water has been absorbed and the rice is tender.

4 Cook the macaroni in a pan of boiling salted water until al dente, about 9–12 minutes or according to instructions on the packet. Transfer the lentils, rice and macaroni to a plate, top with half the crispy onions and gently mix. Ladle the tomato sauce on top, followed by the garlic vinaigrette. Sprinkle with the parsley and scatter over the remaining onions. Serve hot.

LINGUINE

With aubergine, fried capers & feta

A simple pasta dish for when you're in need of a carb-fix before falling asleep in front of the TV. Fried capers are powerful pops of crunchy, salty goodness with which you can adorn your food, including salads and soups – make a big batch as they keep really well.

2 small aubergines

Vegetable oil, for deep-frying

50g (1¾oz) capers, drained and rinsed

90ml (3fl oz) olive oil, plus extra if needed and to serve

1 red onion, finely chopped

2 garlic cloves, grated

500g (1lb 2oz) cherry tomatoes

1 tsp sugar (optional)

½ bunch of basil, leaves picked

320g (11½oz) linguine

40g (1½oz) feta, crumbled

Small handful of Crispy Sourdough Breadcrumbs (page 188)

Grated zest of 1 lemon

Flaked sea salt

1 Cut each aubergine lengthways into quarters and cut each quarter into 5cm (2in) wedges. Toss the aubergine wedges in salt and place in a colander set over a sink for 45 minutes. Rinse under running water and squeeze dry.

2 Pour enough oil to come up the sides of a deep saucepan by 2–2.5cm (¾–1in) and set over medium until hot (roughly 180°C/350°F if you have a thermometer probe to hand). Deep-fry the capers for 1–2 minutes until crisp and slightly curled up at the sides. Lift the capers from the oil using a slotted spoon and transfer to a plate lined with kitchen paper. Set aside until required.

3 Heat the olive oil in a wide, shallow frying pan and set over medium heat until just shimmering but not smoking. Add the aubergine and fry, flipping halfway, for 5–7 minutes or until golden brown on both sides and completely tender. Use a slotted spoon and transfer the aubergine to a bowl lined with kitchen paper and season with salt. Top up the pan with some olive oil if necessary, add the onion and cook for 5–7 minutes or until softened and translucent. Add the garlic and continue to cook for a few minutes before throwing in the cherry tomatoes. Season with salt and cook over medium-low heat, stirring occasionally, for 20–25 minutes until the tomatoes have burst, released their juices and reduced a little. Check for seasoning; you may need to add sugar.

4 Gently add the aubergines to the pan and continue to cook over low heat for a further 7–10 minutes. Be careful not to move the aubergine too much as you want them to hold their shape. A few minutes prior to the end of cooking, add the basil leaves, reserving a few for garnish, and allow to gently wilt.

5 Meanwhile, bring a large pan of salted water to the boil over high heat, add the linguine and cook until al dente, according to the packet instructions. Using a pair of tongs or a slotted spoon, transfer the linguine to the sauce, add some of the capers, feta and crispy breadcrumbs (reserving a handful of each for the garnish) and toss together. Cook for a further 2 minutes.

6 Transfer the linguine to serving plates, top with any remaining fried capers, feta and breadcrumbs, as well as the lemon zest liberally sprinkled all over. Finish with a drizzle of olive oil and reserved basil leaves.

LEEK DUMPLINGS

Manti, or mantu, a type of dumpling popular in Turkish and Balkan cuisine, is similar, in essence, to ravioli, and every bit as labour intensive. I've used gyoza wrappers because it makes the process that much easier, and ultimately far less intimidating, meaning there's more chance that you'll have a go at making it.

YOGHURT SAUCE
250g (9oz) Greek yoghurt
1½ tbsp dried mint
2 garlic cloves, minced
1 tbsp lemon juice
Flaked sea salt and ground
    black pepper

TOMATO SAUCE
120g (4½oz) tomato paste
40ml (1¼fl oz) olive oil
½ tbsp Aleppo chilli flakes
    (pul biber)
150ml (5fl oz) water
Pinch of sugar, to taste

LEEK DUMPLINGS
100ml (3½fl oz) extra-virgin
    olive oil, plus extra to
    drizzle
5 spring onions, sliced
3 leeks, white and light
    green parts only, thinly
    sliced and rinsed
2 garlic cloves, grated or
    minced
2 tsp dried chilli flakes
1 tbsp grated lemon zest
Small bunch of flat-leaf
    parsley, finely chopped
40 gyoza wrappers
½ tbsp sumac, to serve
Small handful of dill, to
    serve

FOR THE YOGHURT SAUCE

❶ Combine all of the ingredients in a bowl and stir well. Season to taste.

FOR THE TOMATO SAUCE

❶ Combine the tomato paste and olive oil in a small saucepan and cook over medium heat for 7–10 minutes, stirring regularly, until rich and caramelized. Add the chilli flakes to the pan and fry for a minute or so, followed by the water, then stir to combine. Bring the sauce to a gentle simmer, turn the heat down to low and simmer for 5–7 minutes until thickened and reduced. Season with salt to taste and check for balance, adding a pinch of sugar as necessary to round off the acidity from the tomato paste. Keep warm until required.

FOR THE LEEK DUMPLINGS

❶ Warm 50ml (1¾fl oz) olive oil in a heavy-based medium frying pan and cook the spring onions and leeks over medium heat, stirring regularly for 7–10 minutes, until softened. Add the garlic and chilli flakes and fry for 1–2 minutes, then throw in the lemon zest and parsley, and stir to combine. Season to taste, set aside to cool slightly then transfer to the fridge for 30 minutes to cool.

❷ Have a bowl of water to hand and hold a gyoza wrapper in the palm of one hand. Wet the edges of the wrapper with water, making a full circle with your finger, so as to moisten it and help the edges to stick once wrapped. Spoon a teaspoon of the stuffing into the centre of each wrapper. Fold one half over the other, hold the dumpling with your right hand, then pinch and pleat the dumpling using your left index finger and thumb, every 5mm (¼in), working from right to left. Repeat with the remaining wrappers and filling. Set aside on a tray dusted with a little flour and refrigerate.

❸ When you are ready to cook the dumplings, bring a large pan of salted water to the boil over high heat, lower the heat to a rolling simmer, add the dumplings, in batches, and cook for 4–5 minutes or until they float to the surface. Lift the dumplings from the water using a slotted spoon and transfer to serving plates Drizzle the tomato sauce over the top, followed by the yoghurt sauce. Garnish with a drizzle of olive oil, sumac sprinkled on top and the dill leaves.

JEWELLED TAHDIG

Tahdig (pronounced tah-deeg) is a Persian dish that translates to 'bottom of the pot', a reference to the crunchy golden-brown layer of rice that forms at the bottom of the pan. Perfecting the technique requires practice, patience and perseverance. This was inspired by a rendition that I ate Kismet, at an outstanding restaurant in Los Angeles.

300ml (10fl oz) verjuice

100g (3½oz) caster sugar

80g (2¾oz) currants

60g (2oz) barberries

80g (2¾oz) pumpkin seeds

40g (1½oz) pistachios

2 tbsp olive oil

1 tbsp flaked sea salt

360g (12½oz) basmati rice

1 bay leaf

1 tbsp fennel seeds

75g (2¾oz) butter, melted, plus extra for greasing

1½ tbsp natural yoghurt

20g (¾oz) rice flour, mixed with cold water to form a slurry paste

2 egg yolks

1 Bring the verjuice and sugar to the boil in a medium-sized saucepan over medium-high heat. Add the currants and barberries. Take off the heat and set aside, allowing the fruit to soak in the juices for 30 minutes – they will soften and plump up. Drain and set aside until required.

2 Preheat the oven to 160°C (275°F)/140°C Fan/Gas Mark 3. Roll the pumpkin seeds and pistachios in the olive oil and season with the salt. Transfer to a parchment-lined baking sheet and toast in the oven for 25–30 minutes until golden and crunchy. Set aside to cool.

3 Rinse the rice in a bowl filled with cold water and swirl several times with your fingers to release the starch. Repeat the process two or three times until the water runs clear. Drain and set aside. Put the bay leaf and fennel seeds on a muslin and tie a knot, making a bouquet garni. Half fill a 20cm (8in) saucepan with water, add the bouquet garni, and bring to the boil over high heat. Add the rice, stir several times, bring back to the boil and cook over medium-high heat for 5 minutes until the rice is slightly softened but still firm. Drain the rice and run under cold water briefly to cool to stop it from cooking any further, then leave to stand in the colander for a few minutes. Transfer to a baking tray, spread out to a thin layer and set aside until completely cooled.

4 Butter a non-stick frying pan. Take one-third of the par-cooked rice and place in a large bowl with the yoghurt, a third of the melted butter and the rice flour slurry. Stir to combine. Spread this rice evenly in a thin layer onto the bottom of the prepared frying pan. This will form the tahdig. Layer the remaining par-cooked rice on top intermittently with three-quarters of the currants, barberries, pumpkin seeds and pistachios (saving the rest for the garnish), working your way up in layers to make a mound shape. Do not pack the rice down. It should be layered lightly to leave space for the rice to expand. Wrap the lid of the pan tightly with a clean tea towel and place on top so that it fits snugly. Place the pan over medium-low heat and cook for 12–15 minutes. Towards the end of cooking, drizzle the rest of the butter around the edges.

5 Just before serving, dig up a small well in the top of the rice and gently add the egg yolks. Cover the yolks with the rice and, using a plate where the lid once was, invert the rice carefully on to a plate. Serve immediately with the rest of the pumpkin seeds, pistachios, raisins and barberries scattered over the top.

10 FRIED

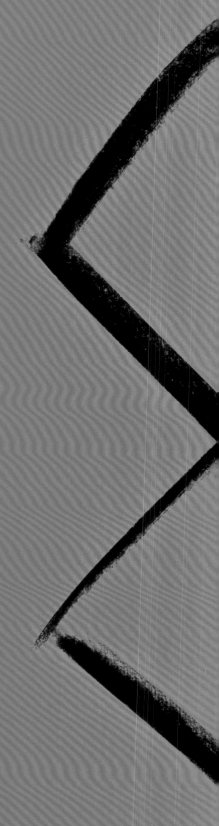

BATTERED

POLENTA-FRIED
JAPANESE AUBERGINE

With lavender honey, fried herbs & Persian lime salt

Japanese aubergines are long and slender, more similar in appearance to the Turkish variety than some of their European counterparts, and therefore more suitable for this particular recipe. If you can't find this variety, feel free to use smaller-sized regular aubergines, bearing in mind the cooking time will need adjusting. Soaking the aubergine in milk is a technique used to remove some of its natural bitterness, but it also results in a creamier texture that contrasts the crunch of the polenta coating perfectly.

LAVENDER HONEY
50g (1¾oz) honey
1 tsp dried lavender

POLENTA-FRIED
AUBERGINE
2 Japanese aubergines,
    sliced into 1cm (½in)
    rounds
400ml (13½fl oz) whole
    milk
25g (1oz) flaked sea salt
1 Persian dried lime or
    1 tsp sumac
1 tsp dried chilli flakes
2 rosemary sprigs, leaves
    picked
10–12 picked sage leaves
Vegetable oil, for shallow-
    frying
60g (2oz) plain flour
3 tbsp polenta
120g (4½ oz) Whipped Feta
    (page 193), or crème
    fraîche

FOR THE LAVENDER HONEY

1 Warm the honey with the lavender in a small saucepan over medium-high heat until very hot. Remove from the heat and set aside to cool down and infuse.

FOR THE POLENTA-FRIED AUBERGINE

1 Soak the sliced aubergine rounds in a bowl with the milk, making sure that each piece is covered. Set aside for a minimum of 2 hours or even overnight.

2 Pulse the salt, Persian lime and chilli flakes in a food processor or pound them together in a mortar and pestle until the consistency of coarse powder.

3 Pour enough oil to come up the sides of a deep saucepan by 5cm (2in) and set over medium until hot (roughly 180°C/350°F). Fry the herbs in the oil for 20–30 seconds, until crisp then transfer to a tray lined with kitchen paper to absorb any excess oil. Season with salt and set aside. Reserve the oil for later use.

4 To fry the aubergine, heat enough oil to come up to 2.5cm (1in) in a frying pan. Strain the aubergine rounds from the milk and pat dry with kitchen paper. Combine the flour and polenta in a bowl. Dredge the aubergine slices in the flour mix until covered on both sides and dust off any excess. Fry in the hot oil in batches, being careful not to overcrowd the pan, for 3–5 minutes or until golden crisp, then transfer to kitchen paper to drain.

5 Spread the whipped feta on the base of a plate and overlap the aubergine slices on top. Add a generous dusting of Persian lime salt, drizzle with lavender honey and garnish with the fried sage and rosemary.

PARSNIP SCHNITZ

I don't know who invented schnitzel, but they deserve a statue to be erected some place in their honour. Universally adored the world over, every country has their own version.

CONFIT GARLIC & CAPER AIOLI

12 Confit Garlic cloves
    (page 193)
2 egg yolks
1 tsp Dijon mustard
60ml (2fl oz) olive oil
60ml (2fl oz) vegetable oil
2½ tbsp lemon juice
1 tsp paprika
30g (1oz) capers, rinsed
    and roughly chopped
50g (1¾oz) sour cream
Flaked sea salt and ground
    black pepper

PARSNIP SCHNITZ

1kg (2lb 3oz) parsnips,
    peeled and halved
60ml (2fl oz) olive oil
2 garlic cloves, smashed,
    skin on
Few thyme sprigs
1 small dried chilli,
    crumbled (or 1 tsp
    dried chilli flakes)
120g (4½oz) Panko
    breadcrumbs
1 tbsp paprika
¾ tbsp ground cumin
100g (3½oz) plain flour
2 eggs, lightly beaten with
    2 tbsp milk
Flaked sea salt and ground
    black pepper

Sunflower or vegetable oil,
    for shallow-frying
2 lemons, cut into quarters

FOR THE CONFIT GARLIC & CAPER AIOLI

1 Put the confit garlic, egg yolks and mustard in a food processor and pulse a few times to combine.

2 Mix the oils together in a jug. Slowly and gradually pour the oil into the food processor bowl while the motor is running – the mixture will thicken and emulsify. Add the lemon juice and paprika and pulse to combine. Season to taste with salt and black pepper. Fold through the capers and as much sour cream as desired – you may not need or wish to use all of it.

FOR THE PARSNIP SCHNITZ

1 Preheat the oven to 200°C (400°F)/180°C Fan/Gas Mark 6.

2 Toss the parsnips with the olive oil, garlic and thyme in a medium bowl. Place a large piece of foil (about 30cm/12in long) on a work surface and cover with a piece of parchment paper. Fold over the edges to secure the parchment paper within the foil and place the parsnips on the paper, with the garlic and thyme sprigs scattered all around and any excess oil still in the bowl drizzled on top. Crumble the dried chilli (or chilli flakes) on top, season with salt and a few grinds of black pepper and fold to enclose, ensuring the foil is tightly crimped so that steam cannot escape. Roast for 45–50 minutes until tender, then remove from the oven, set aside to cool and discard the inner core.

3 Combine the breadcrumbs with the paprika, ground cumin and 1½ teaspoons salt. Dredge the parsnips in the flour, shaking off any excess, then dip each piece into the beaten eggs and milk mixture and lastly roll in the spiced breadcrumb to coat. Transfer each piece to a tray as you work.

4 In a deep frying pan, pour oil up to 1cm (½in) in depth, and set over medium-high heat. Carefully lower each piece of parsnip into the pan and shallow-fry on both sides for 3–5 minutes, until golden brown. Remove with a slotted spoon and transfer to a plate lined with kitchen paper to absorb any excess oil.

5 Serve the parsnip with lemon wedges for squeezing over the top and the confit garlic aioli alongside for dipping in.

SCRAMBLED EGG BREAKFAST BUN

With tomato-chilli jam, harissa aioli & halloumi

his is a decadent breakfast bun that will probably give you a heart attack. But, if you do
e, at least you'll die happy.

small red onion, sliced

g (2¾oz) cherry
  tomatoes, quartered

g (⅓oz) flat-leaf parsley,
  leaves picked

tbsp extra-virgin olive
  oil

bsp lemon juice

sp sumac

0ml (3½fl oz) sunflower
  oil, for frying

bsp plain flour

halloumi cheese,
  200–250g (7–9oz), cut
  into 4 slices

arge eggs

g (2oz) unsalted butter

spring onion, thinly
  sliced

(¼oz) coriander, finely
  chopped

bsp Tomato-chilli Jam
  (page 189)

bsp Harissa Aioli (page
  191) or see Tip

rioche buns, toasted

aked sea salt and coarse
  black pepper

❶ Preheat the oven to 120°C (250°F)/100°C Fan/Gas Mark ½.

❷ Combine the onion, tomatoes and parsley in a small bowl, add the olive oil,
lemon juice and sumac, and season to taste with salt and pepper. Set aside.

❸ Warm the sunflower oil in a non-stick frying pan over medium-high heat.
Season the flour well with salt and pepper. Pat the halloumi slices dry with
kitchen paper, dredge in the flour, shaking off any excess and fry in for 1–1½
minutes on both sides, until golden brown and crisp. Lift the halloumi using a
slotted spoon to a plate lined with kitchen paper to absorb any excess oil, then
place on a tray and transfer to the oven to keep warm while you get on with
making the eggs.

❹ Crack the eggs into a cold, wide, non-stick frying pan and whisk to combine
the yolks and whites. Drop the butter into the pan and place over medium-low
heat. Using a spatula, turn and fold the eggs continuously until the butter has
been incorporated into the eggs and they are light and fluffy but still moist. Do
not stop folding the eggs over. Season with salt and black pepper, remove
from the heat and fold through the spring onion and coriander.

❺ Cut the brioche buns in half and spread a layer of tomato-chilli jam on the base
and the harissa aioli on the top half. Place the scrambled eggs on the bottom
bun, then the pan-fried halloumi on top. Layer on the red onion and tomato
salad and serve immediately while piping hot.

TIP   If you're short on time, simply mix some harissa with
             mayonnaise.

RED PEPPER BRIK

With spinach & egg

Brik (or breek) is a North African dish made by stuffing paper-thin pastry and deep-frying it, similar in concept to a spring roll. Who doesn't love deep-fried crispy pastry that's been stuffed with things? Nobody.

FILLING BASE

3 red peppers, halved, deseeded and cut into 1cm (½in) strips
2 red onions, each cut into 6 or 8 wedges
1 red chilli, thinly sliced
1 tsp ground cumin
2 or 3 thyme sprigs, leaves picked
100ml (3½fl oz) olive oil
2 garlic cloves, thinly sliced
200g (7oz) baby spinach
Pinch of ground nutmeg
Flaked sea salt and coarse black pepper

BRIK

4 circles feuilles de brick pastry (or filo pastry)
2 tbsp chopped flat-leaf parsley
4 eggs
1 egg white, lightly beaten
Sunflower oil, for deep-frying
2 tbsp date syrup, mixed with 1 tbsp lukewarm water (optional)

❶ Preheat the oven to 180°C (350°F)/160°Fan/Gas Mark 4. Toss the sliced peppers with the onions, chilli, cumin, thyme and 70ml (2¼fl oz) of the olive oil in a medium bowl. Season generously with salt and black pepper and transfer to a parchment-lined baking sheet. Roast in the preheated oven for 35–40 minutes, stirring a couple of times during cooking, until softened and just charred round the edges. Remove and set aside to cool.

❷ Meanwhile, heat the rest of the olive oil in a frying pan over medium heat, add the garlic and cook for 2–3 minutes or until the garlic has just started to colour. Throw the spinach into the pan, and allow to wilt. Season with salt, pepper and nutmeg, and add to the pepper and onion mixture.

❸ Working one at a time, spread out a pastry leaf (keeping the rest covered with a damp tea towel so they don't dry out) and place a quarter of the peppers and spinach mix on one half of the leaf, followed by ½ tablespoon flat-leaf parsley. Carefully break an egg over the top, ensuring the yolk does not break, season generously and fold the pastry leaf over to form a semi-circle (or triangle). Seal the edges with the egg white then crimp and fold the edges back over themselves for a stronger seal. Repeat with the remaining pastry.

❹ Pour enough oil to come up the side of a deep saucepan by 2–2.5cm (¾–1in) and set over medium heat until hot (roughly 180°C/350°F if you have a thermometer probe to hand). Gently slide the briks into the oil one at a time and fry for 1½–2 minutes, spooning the hot oil over the top, until golden brown all over. Carefully lift the brik pastry from the oil, transfer to a tray lined with kitchen paper and keep warm while you repeat the process. Serve brushed (or drizzled) with date syrup (if using).

VARIATION Date syrup provides a lovely sweet glaze here. You could use honey, or nothing at all. A dollop of crème fraîche to serve wouldn't go amiss.

STUFFED
COURGETTE FLOWERS

With saffron aioli

Courgette flowers come around for only a few weeks every summer. Blink and you might miss them, which would be a shame, because they're worth traipsing around your entire city trying to find them. I can think of no better way to treat a courgette flower than to stuff and deep-fry it. It's what Mother Earth intended them for.

200g (7oz) ricotta

100g (3½oz) soft goat's cheese

1 tbsp picked lemon thyme

5g (¼oz) chives, finely sliced

1 tbsp finely grated lemon zest

12 large courgette flowers

120g (4½oz) plain flour

50g (1¾oz) cornflour

1 tsp baking powder

225ml (7½fl oz) iced sparkling mineral water

sunflower oil, for deep-frying

4 tbsp Saffron Aioli (page 193)

1 lemon, quartered

flaked sea salt and ground black pepper

1 Whip the ricotta and goat's cheese in a mixing bowl with a whisk until smooth, then fold through the lemon thyme, chives and lemon zest. Season to taste with salt and several grinds of black pepper. Carefully spoon (or pipe) the mixture into each courgette flower, roughly 1 tablespoon per flower.

2 Sift the flour, cornflour and baking powder together in a large bowl and season with ¾ teaspoon salt. Gradually pour in the iced sparkling water and whisk until the batter is light and aerated, and the consistency of single cream. Season with 1 teaspoon flaked salt and several grinds of black pepper.

3 Pour enough sunflower oil to come up to 12–15cm (5–6in) in a deep, heavy-based frying pan and set over medium-high heat until the temperature reaches 180°C (350°F) – or use a deep-fryer with a thermometer dial.

4 Working in batches, dip the courgette flowers into the batter and carefully lower each one into the hot oil. Fry in a few batches, for 2–3 minutes, rolling them gently with a slotted spoon so that they cook evenly, until golden brown all over. Lift the flowers from the oil, transfer to a plate lined with kitchen paper and keep warm while you fry the remaining flowers.

5 Distribute three courgette flowers to each plate, season with flaked salt over the top and serve with a dollop of saffron aioli on the side and a wedge of lemon for squeezing over the top. Serve immediately while piping hot.

TIP   For some entirely optional added sweetness, drizzle some Lavender Honey (page 172) over just before serving. A chilli-infused honey would work brilliantly too, or just use a best-quality runny honey instead.

BUTTERMILK-FRIED CAULIFLOWER

With mint yoghurt dip

This is a bit like a vegetarian fritto misto. You could add other vegetables to the mix, such as fennel, thinly sliced squash or leeks, or substitute out the cauliflower altogether.

MINT YOGHURT DIP
200g (7oz) Greek yoghurt
1 shallot, finely chopped
2 tbsp capers, rinsed and
    roughly chopped
2 garlic cloves, minced
2 tbsp picked mint leaves,
    roughly chopped
1 tbsp grated lemon zest
1½ tbsp lemon juice
1½ tsp dried mint
1½ tbsp olive oil
Flaked sea salt

BUTTERMILK-FRIED CAULIFLOWER
400ml (13½fl oz) buttermilk
1½ tsp ground cumin
1 tsp ground cinnamon
½ tsp ground turmeric
1 cauliflower, cut into
    florets
200g (7oz) plain flour
½ tbsp salt
1 tsp ground black pepper
1 lemon, thinly sliced to
    3mm (⅛in) rounds
Vegetable oil, for frying
Few picked sage leaves
½ tbsp nutritional yeast
    (optional)

FOR THE MINT YOGHURT DIP

1 Combine the yoghurt, shallot, capers and garlic together in a small bowl and stir to combine. Pound the mint with a spoonful of water in a mortar and pestle until well broken down and add it to the yoghurt. Add the lemon zest, juice, dried mint and olive oil. Give the dip a good mix, and season to taste with salt.

FOR THE BUTTERMILK-FRIED CAULIFLOWER

1 In a bowl, combine the buttermilk, spices and cauliflower florets. Set aside to marinate for a minimum of 1 hour or overnight.

2 Pour enough oil to come up the sides of a deep saucepan by 2–2.5cm (¾–1in) and set over medium heat until hot (roughly 180°C/350°F).

3 Sift the flour with the salt and black pepper. Dredge the cauliflower and lemon slices in the flour, tossing to coat, then dip them back into the buttermilk and roll in the flour once more. Deep-fry the cauliflower, in batches so as to not overcrowd the pan, tossing frequently for about 5 minutes or until golden brown and crunchy. Carefully transfer to plate lined with kitchen paper, using a slotted spoon. Taste for seasoning and season with flaked salt if desired. Quickly fry the sage leaves, over medium-high heat, for no more than 30 seconds until just crisp, tossing in the oil as they cook. Remove from the oil with a slotted spoon and transfer to kitchen paper to drain.

4 Serve immediately, still piping hot, with the sage leaves strewn over, dusted with nutritional yeast flakes (if using) and the mint yoghurt served alongside.

SWEETCORN FRITTERS

With slow-roasted tomatoes & Persian lime yoghurt

Sweetcorn fritters have been on the menu of every self-respecting Antipodean café long before we'd even heard of smashed avocado on toast. I've gone for slow-roasted tomatoes and Persian lime yoghurt, but use the fritters as your base and load them as you wish.

PERSIAN LIME YOGHURT

150g (5½oz) Greek yoghurt
1 garlic clove, minced
1 Persian lime, grated
1 tbsp lime juice
2 tbsp chives, finely sliced
1 tbsp olive oil
Flaked sea salt and ground
    black pepper

SWEETCORN FRITTERS

120g (4½oz) plain flour
1 tsp baking powder
1 tbsp ground cumin
¾ tsp ground turmeric
1 tbsp caster sugar
2 eggs
100ml (3½fl oz) milk
1 red onion, chopped
1 red pepper, finely diced
20g (¾oz) coriander
    leaves, chopped, plus
    extra to garnish
1 garlic clove, minced
2 corn-on-the-cobs,
    kernels cut off
1½ tsp salt
¾ tsp black pepper
Sunflower oil, for frying
8 Slow-roasted Tomatoes
    (page 194)
1 bunch of rocket
2 tbsp olive oil

FOR THE PERSIAN LIME YOGHURT

1 Combine all of the ingredients in a mixing bowl and whisk well to incorporate. Season to taste with salt and ground black pepper.

FOR THE SWEETCORN FRITTERS

1 Sift the flour and baking powder into a large bowl and add the spices and sugar. Whisk the eggs and milk together in a small bowl, and add the mixture to the flour, whisking to make a smooth batter.

2 In a separate bowl, combine the red onion, red pepper, coriander, garlic, corn, salt and pepper, then add this to the batter to bind.

3 In a wide, heavy-based frying pan, pour sunflower oil up to 2cm (¾in) in depth and set over high heat until very hot. Working in batches, carefully drop the sweetcorn mixture into the oil, roughly 2 tablespoons per fritter. Fry the fritters for 4–5 minutes, until golden on both sides, adjusting the heat if need be so that the fritters don't burn on the outside before the batter has cooked all the way through to the middle. Lift the fritters from the pan using a slotted spoon, transfer to a plate lined with kitchen paper and keep warm in the oven set to its lowest heat. Continue to fry the rest of the sweetcorn batter.

4 Distribute the fritters onto serving plates stacked on top of one another, sprinkle with salt, drizzle with Persian lime yoghurt, top with slow-roasted tomatoes and garnish with any reserved coriander leaves. Dress the rocket with olive oil and serve alongside. Eat while piping hot or warm.

BEETROOT & CARROT ROSTI

With cardamom yoghurt & chickpeas

This is a great option for a lazy Sunday brunch. These rosti are quick, easy and a perfect remedy for any lingering hangover. Add some Tomato-chilli Jam (page 189) if you have some, for an extra kick, and a poached egg wouldn't go amiss here either.

CARDAMOM YOGHURT
120g (4½oz) Greek yoghurt
80g (2¾oz) crème fraîche
1 tsp ground cardamom
Grated zest of 1 lime
1 tbsp olive oil
Flaked sea salt and ground
    black pepper

**BEETROOT & CARROT
ROSTI**
2 beetroot, peeled
2 carrots, peeled
1 large sweet potato,
    peeled
1 spring onion, sliced
2 garlic cloves, grated or
    minced
2 tbsp finely chopped dill
60g (2oz) plain flour
2 eggs, lightly beaten
120g (4½oz) feta, crumbled
50ml (1¾fl oz) olive oil

GARNISH
200g (7oz) tinned
    chickpeas
2 tbsp lemon juice
50ml (1¾fl oz) olive oil
Handful of coriander
    leaves
1 lime, cut into 4 wedges

FOR THE CARDAMOM YOGHURT AND GARNISH

1 Mix all of the ingredients together in a bowl and whisk to incorporate. Check for seasoning and adjust according to taste.

2 Drain the chickpeas and rinse well. Put in a bowl with the lemon juice and olive oil. Season with salt and a few grinds of pepper and leave to marinate while you make the rosti.

FOR THE BEETROOT & CARROT ROSTI

1 Coarsely grate the beetroot, carrots and sweet potato into a mixing bowl and season liberally with salt. Set aside over a colander for 30 minutes and transfer to a cheesecloth or kitchen paper, then wring the grated vegetables dry as much as possible. Add the spring onion, garlic and dill to the bowl, season with pepper and mix well. Sift the flour into the bowl, then add the eggs. Add the feta, folding it through thoroughly to ensure it is well mixed.

2 Heat the olive oil in a pan over medium heat, take a large spoonful of the mixture and shape it into a patty, then lower it carefully into the hot oil. Depending on the size of the pan, you should be able to fry 3–4 rosti at a time but be careful not to overcrowd the pan. Shallow-fry for 4–5 minutes, or until golden and crisp on both sides. Transfer to kitchen paper and repeat the frying with the remaining mixture.

3 Transfer the rosti to serving plates, top with a generous dollop of cardamom yoghurt, followed by the marinated chickpeas, and finish with some coriander to garnish and a lime wedge for squeezing.

11 CONDIMENTS

LARDER

CRISPY SOURDOUGH BREADCRUMBS

Makes about
250g (9oz)

220g (8oz) 2–3 day old
    sourdough, crusts
    removed
50ml (1¾fl oz) olive oil
2 garlic cloves, minced
1 tbsp dried chilli flakes
Grated zest of 1 lemon
Flaked sea salt and ground
    black pepper

1 Blitz the bread in a food processor to a coarse crumb.

2 Heat the olive oil in a shallow frying pan over medium heat and add the garlic and chilli flakes to infuse, frying for 10–15 seconds while stirring continuously, then add the breadcrumbs and fry for about 5 minutes until golden brown.

3 Transfer the breadcrumbs to some kitchen paper to soak up any excess oil, stir through the lemon zest and season with salt and black pepper to taste. Stored in an airtight container, these will last for 3–5 days.

PISTACHIO DUKKAH

Makes about
175g (6oz)

25g (1oz) coriander seeds,
    toasted
30g (1oz) cumin seeds,
    toasted
15g (½oz) fennel seeds,
    toasted
80g (2¾oz) pistachios,
    toasted
2 tbsp nigella seeds,
    toasted
2 tbsp sesame seeds,
    toasted
1½ tsp flaked sea salt
Freshly ground black
    pepper

1 Blitz the coriander, cumin and fennel seeds together in a food processor, or preferably a spice grinder, being careful not to over-blend. Remove and set aside in a bowl.

2 Process the pistachios in the same way, avoiding grinding them for too long otherwise they will turn into an oily paste – you're after a coarsely ground crumb. Add the pistachios to the bowl with the ground seeds and fold through the nigella and sesame seeds and the salt. Season with pepper. Stored in an airtight container the dukkah will keep for several months.

TOMATO-CHILLI JAM

Makes
~~00~~–600g (1lb
~~oz~~–1lb 5oz)

tsp yellow mustard
   seeds
~~2~~ tsp coriander seeds
~~3~~ tsp cumin seeds
~~8~~00g (1lb 12oz) Slow-
   roasted Tomatoes
   (page 194)
garlic cloves, finely
   chopped or minced
bird's-eye chillies,
   deseeded and chopped
red chillies, deseeded
   and chopped
½ tbsp fish sauce
~~1~~00ml (3½fl oz) red wine
   vinegar
~~1~~60g (5½oz) light brown
   sugar

1 Toast the mustard, coriander and cumin seeds together in a small frying pan until fragrant and just starting to pop, then transfer to a pestle and mortar and crush to a fine blend. (You could also use a spice grinder for this step.)

2 Combine the tomatoes, garlic, chillies and fish sauce in a food processor and blend to a rough paste. Transfer the paste to a heavy-based medium-sized saucepan and add the toasted ground seeds, the red wine vinegar and sugar. Bring to the boil, then reduce the heat to very low and cook gently for 1–1½ hours, stirring regularly to prevent the jam from catching, until the jam is thickened to the point it leaves a trail when you to run a spoon across the base of the pan. Take off the heat and allow to cool briefly.

3 Transfer to a jar or airtight container where it will keep in the fridge for several weeks, or in a sterilized jar in a dark, cool place for up to 3 months.

TOMATO & POMEGRANATE DRESSING

Makes about
~~3~~00g (10½oz)

~~2~~ shallots, finely chopped
   garlic clove, minced
~~2~~50g (9oz) tomatoes,
   deseeded and finely
   diced
~~3~~0g (1oz) pomegranate
   seeds
½ tbsp pomegranate
   molasses
½ tbsp red wine vinegar
~~8~~0ml (2½fl oz) extra-virgin
   olive oil
Flaked sea salt and ground
   black pepper

1 Combine the shallots, garlic, tomatoes and pomegranate in a bowl. Add the pomegranate molasses, red wine vinegar and olive oil. Whisk well to combine, taste for seasoning and adjust accordingly with salt and black pepper.

SAFFRON WATER

Makes 150ml
(5fl oz)

Large pinch of saffron
strands, about 50
150ml (5fl oz) boiling water

1. In a small bowl, cover the saffron strands with boiling water and set aside to infuse for a minimum of 15 minutes, preferably an hour. The saffron water can be made well in advance and stored for later use.

HERB OIL

Makes about
200ml (7fl oz)

Small bunch of chives
20g (¾oz) coriander
20g (¾oz) flat-leaf parsley
280ml (9½fl oz) olive oil

1. Place the herbs and olive oil in a food processor or blender. Blitz the herbs for 4–5 minutes, or until completely smooth. Transfer the herb oil to a large, clean piece of muslin (cheese) cloth (or some overlapping J-cloths as an alternative), tie the four corners together and hang over a bowl positioned underneath (see method for Labneh, opposite). The oil should be a dark, vibrant green. Stored in an airtight jar this will keep for 3–4 days.

SUMAC YOGHURT

Makes about
240g (8½oz)

150g (5½oz) Greek yoghurt
1 garlic clove, minced
1 tbsp sumac
2 tbsp lemon juice
2 tbsp olive oil
Flaked sea salt and ground
black pepper

1. Combine all the ingredients together in bowl and stir well.

LABNEH

Makes about
500g (1lb 2oz)

500g (1lb 2oz) full-fat
    natural yoghurt
1 tsp salt

1 Season the yoghurt with the salt and stir to combine. Spoon the yoghurt into a muslin (cheese) cloth – or several J-cloths overlaid on one another – and hang, if possible. (I like to tie the cloth in a bundle affixed to the spout of my kitchen tap, enabling the whey to deposit in the sink below.) Alternatively, set the cloth in a colander or strainer with a bowl underneath to collect the whey.

2 Allow the labneh to strain for as long as the desired consistency demands. Within 12–24 hours it will yield a labneh with quite a loose and creamy consistency, whereas any longer will produce a drier and more crumbly-textured result.

HARISSA CRÈME FRAÎCHE

Makes about
220g (8oz)

160g (5½oz) crème fraîche
40g (1½oz) rose harissa or
    harissa
1 tbsp olive oil
Flaked sea salt and ground
    black pepper

1 Combine all the ingredients in a medium-sized bowl and stir to combine. Taste for seasoning and adjust accordingly. Keeps for 3–5 days in an airtight container, refrigerated.

HARISSA AIOLI

Makes about
250g (9oz)

2 egg yolks
2 garlic cloves, minced
200ml (7fl oz) olive oil
30g (1oz) rose harissa or
    harissa
Flaked sea salt

1 Put the egg yolks, garlic and a good pinch of salt in a food processor and blend to combine.

2 Slowly pour in the olive oil, being careful to keep it a slow and steady stream so that the aioli does not split, until the mixture has emulsified and thickened. Add the harissa and pulse to combine. Season with salt to taste.

SAFFRON AIOLI

Makes about
[...]00g (10½oz)

[...] egg yolks
[...] garlic cloves, minced
[¼] tsp salt
[...]75ml (6fl oz) olive oil
[...]e tbsp lemon juice
[...]cant 1½ tbsp Saffron
    Water (page 190)
[f]laked sea salt

① Put the egg yolks, garlic and salt in a food processor and blitz to combine.

② Slowly pour in the oil, being careful to keep it a slow and steady stream so that the aioli does not split, until the mixture has emulsified and thickened. Add the lemon juice and saffron water and pulse to combine. Season with salt to taste.

WHIPPED FETA

Makes about
[...]75g (13oz)

[...]30g (4½oz) feta
[1]00g (3½oz) crème fraîche
[...] garlic clove, minced
[...]e tsp Dijon mustard
[g]round black pepper

① Place the feta in a medium-sized bowl filled with water and soak for 10–15 minutes, which will help remove any excess salt. Drain the feta and then repeat the process all over again.

② Process the feta in a blender with the crème fraîche, garlic and mustard until completely smooth. You may need to stop once or twice to push down any lumps that get stuck on the sides. Finish with a few grinds of black pepper.

CONFIT GARLIC & HERB OIL

Makes about
[...]50g (5½oz)

[...] large garlic bulbs, cloves
    separated and peeled
[a]bout 400ml (13½fl oz)
    olive oil, to cover
[...] lemon thyme sprigs
[...] rosemary sprigs
[...] bay leaves

① Preheat the oven to 150°C (300°F)/130°C Fan/Gas Mark 2. Place the garlic cloves in an ovenproof pan with a tight-fitting lid, or else use a roasting pan. Pour over enough olive oil to cover, and throw in the lemon thyme, rosemary and bay leaves. Put the lid on the pan (or cover the roasting pan with crimped foil) and confit the garlic for 45–50 minutes, or until completely softened and caramelized.

② Transfer the garlic to a jar or airtight container, along with the oil to completely submerge, and keep refrigerated until needed. This will keep for a month.

Makes about
550g (1lb 3oz)

SLOW-ROASTED TOMATOES

500g (1lb12oz) plum
    tomatoes, peeled and
    halved
1 garlic clove, thinly sliced
Small bunch of thyme
100ml (3½fl oz) extra-virgin
    olive oil
Flaked sea salt and ground
    black pepper

❶ Preheat the oven to 140°C (280°F)/120°C Fan/Gas Mark 2. Lay the tomato halves cut-side up on a roasting pan, place a slice of garlic in the well of each half and sprinkle some picked thyme leaves over the top. Drizzle the olive oil over each tomato. Season liberally with flaked salt and a pinch of black pepper.

❷ Roast the tomatoes for 1½ hours, or until shrivelled but still retaining texture. Store in an airtight container or jar, covered in oil, in the fridge for 2–3 weeks.

Makes about
550g (1lb 3oz)

CONFIT CHERRY TOMATOES

500g (1lb 2oz) cherry
    tomatoes, peeled
550ml (18½fl oz) olive oil
4–5 garlic cloves, smashed
4–5 thyme sprigs
4–5 oregano sprigs
2 or 3 bay leaves

❶ Preheat the oven to 180°C (350°F)/160°C Fan/Gas Mark 4. Place the tomatoes in a roasting pan and pour over the olive oil to completely cover. Add the garlic and herbs, and cover the pan tightly with foil crimped at the edges.

❷ Roast the tomatoes for 45 minutes to an hour, until tender but not falling apart. Allow to cool and store in an airtight container or jar, covered in the oil, for up to 10 days.

CONFIT CHILLI EZME

300g (10½oz) red chillies
400–500ml (13½–17fl oz)
    olive oil, to cover
lemon thyme sprigs
large garlic cloves,
    unpeeled
bay leaf
flaked sea salt

1 Preheat the oven to 150°C (300°F)/130°C Fan/Gas Mark 2. Place the chillies in an overproof pan with a tight-fitting lid, or else use a roasting pan. Pour over enough olive oil to cover, and throw in the lemon thyme, garlic and bay leaf. Put the lid on the pan (or cover the roasting pan with crimped foil) and confit the chillies for 35–45 minutes, until completely softened and caramelized. Remove from the oven and set aside to cool.

2 Once cooled, remove the chillies from the pan (reserving the chilli-infused oil for later use) and chop them as finely as you can. Pop the garlic from their skins and chop them up too. Add to the chillies and stir to combine. Spoon the chilli ezme into a jar or airtight container, season with salt and cover with the reserved oil. This will keep refrigerated for up to 1 week.

CHILLI SAUCE

400g (14oz) red chillies,
    finely chopped
garlic cloves, finely
    chopped
tsp table salt, plus extra
    to taste
0ml (1¼fl oz) white wine
    vinegar
0g (1½oz) caster sugar

1 Place the chillies and garlic in a 250g (9oz) capacity jar or container, sprinkle with salt and give them a good mix. Put the lid on securely. Set the chillies aside on a shelf to ferment for 3 days, stirring periodically and turning the jar upside-down halfway through. The chillies will start to break down.

2 Warm the vinegar in a small saucepan over medium heat, then add the sugar and stir to dissolve.

3 Transfer the fermented chillies to a food processor and blitz with the vinegar mixture until smooth. Season with salt to taste, decant into a bottle and refrigerate until required. The sauce should keep for 4–5 days, if not longer.

BERBER&Q: ON VEGETABLES

GREEN HARISSA

Makes about
300g (10½oz)

5 Thai green chillies,
    deseeded and roughly
    chopped
3 garlic cloves, minced
2 tbsp capers, drained
1 tsp salt
½ tsp cumin seeds,
    toasted
½ tsp coriander seeds,
    toasted
½ tsp fennel seeds
½ tbsp lemon juice, plus
    extra to taste
25g (1oz) coriander
25g (1oz) flat-leaf parsley
50ml (1¾fl oz) olive oil
½ tbsp honey
Flaked sea salt and ground
    black pepper

1 Combine the chillies, garlic, capers and salt in a mortar and pestle , and pound to a rough paste.

2 Add the seeds and lemon juice, and continue to pound until incorporated. Add the coriander and flat-leaf parsley and continue to pound, gradually adding the olive oil. The harissa will be thick and chunky and you may not need all of the oil. Stir through the honey and check for seasoning, adding more salt or lemon juice if necessary.

S'CHUG

Makes about
250g (9oz)

3 green chillies,
    2 deseeded, roughly
    chopped
3 garlic cloves, roughly
    chopped
3 cardamom pods,
    crushed, husks
    discarded, seeds only
1 bunch of flat-leaf parsley
1 bunch of coriander,
    including stalks (ends
    trimmed)
½ tsp ground cumin
¾ tsp salt
80ml (2½fl oz) extra-virgin
    olive oil
1 tbsp water
Juice of 1 lemon

1 Combine all the ingredients, except the lemon juice, in a food processor, and pulse to combine. The s'chug should remain quite chunky and coarse, so don't blend until smooth. Fold the lemon juice through just prior to serving and check for seasoning.

Makes about
320g (11½ oz)

BASIC TAHINA SAUCE

150g (5½oz) tahini paste
1 tbsp lemon juice
150ml (5fl oz) iced water
Flaked sea salt

1 Pour the tahini into a medium-sized bowl and whisk in the lemon juice. The tahini will thicken at first to a very coarse paste, but don't be put off.

2 Gradually pour in the iced water, whisking as you pour, until the tahini loosens to the consistency of thick cream. Season to taste with salt. Keeps for 3–5 days in an airtight container.

Makes about
360g (12½oz)

ROSE HARISSA TAHINA

40g (1½oz) rose harissa

1 Simply add the rose harissa (or normal harissa if you can't find any) to the basic tahina sauce recipe (above) and fold through to incorporate.

Makes about
350g (12½oz)

GREEN TAHINA

Handful each of picked
    flat-leaf parsley,
    coriander and rocket
    leaves
150ml (5fl oz) water
Juice of 1 lemon, plus
    extra to taste
150g (5½oz) tahini paste
1 garlic clove, minced
Extra-virgin olive oil
Flaked sea salt

1 Blend the herbs and water in a food processor until smooth.

2 Whisk together the lemon juice, tahini and garlic in a bowl, then slowly add a small amount of the herbed water, whisking to combine. The tahini will start to thicken to a rough cement-like paste, but it will loosen as you gradually pour in and combine the remaining herbed water. Season with salt, extra-virgin olive oil and more lemon juice if needed. Stored sealed in the fridge, green tahina will keep for up to 3 days.

AMBA TAHINA

Makes about
350g (12½oz)

30g (1oz) amba

❶ Simply add the amba to the basic tahina sauce recipe (page 199) and fold through to incorporate.

CONFIT SHALLOTS

Makes about
800g (1lb 12oz)

4 or 5 shallots, peeled and
cut in half lengthways
750ml (25½fl oz) olive oil,
plus extra to cover
4–5 garlic cloves, smashed
4 rosemary sprigs

❶ Preheat the oven to 180°C (350°F)/160°C Fan/Gas Mark 4.

❷ Place the shallots in a roasting pan and pour over the olive oil to completely cover. Add the garlic and rosemary and cover the pan tightly with foil crimped at the edges. Confit the shallots for 30–35 minutes in the oven, until tender but not falling apart.

❸ Store in an airtight container, covered in oil, in the fridge for 3–4 weeks.

CRISPY SHALLOTS

Makes about
80g (2¾oz)

400ml (13½fl oz) vegetable
oil
600g (1lb 5oz) shallots,
thinly sliced
Salt

❶ Warm the oil in a small saucepan over medium-low heat until just shimmering, then add the shallots and fry, stirring regularly, for 15–20 minutes until the shallots are golden-brown.

❷ Strain the shallots from the oil using a slotted spoon or spider (reserving the oil for later use) and transfer to a plate lined with kitchen paper to absorb any excess oil. Season the crispy shallots with salt and store in an airtight container, where they can be kept for up to 5 days.

PICKLED RED ONIONS

400ml (13½fl oz) water
200ml (7fl oz) red wine
   vinegar
star anise
cloves
thyme sprigs
bay leaf
30g (1oz) caster sugar
½ tbsp salt
500g (1lb 2oz) red onions,
   thinly sliced

1 Combine all the ingredients except the onions in a medium saucepan. Bring to the boil over medium-high heat, reduce the heat and simmer for 4–5 minutes, until the sugar and salt have dissolved. Remove the pan from the heat and set aside to cool to room temperature.

2 Transfer the sliced onions to a sterilized jar and pour the pickling liquor over the top to cover the onions. The pickle will be ready to eat in 1 hour, but the flavours will intensify and become more complex if given more time. Kept refrigerated, the pickled onions will keep for up to 3 weeks.

PICKLED FENNEL & ORANGE

fennel bulbs, trimmed
   and finely sliced
Zest of 2 oranges, cut
   into strips
bird's-eye chillies, cut in
   half lengthways
300ml (10fl oz) cider
   vinegar
100ml (3½fl oz) water
50g (2oz) fresh ginger,
   grated
80g (2¾oz) soft brown
   sugar
tsp salt
¼ tsp Aleppo chilli flakes
   (pul biber)
Small handful of picked dill
   leaves

1 Combine all the ingredients except the dill in a medium saucepan and bring to the boil over medium-high heat. Reduce the heat to a gentle simmer and poach the fennel for 5 minutes, until the sugar has completely dissolved. Remove from the heat and set aside to cool, then add the dill.

2 Transfer the pickle to a sterilized jar, packing the fennel and aromatics in and pouring the liquid over the top. The pickle will be ready within 3 days but will intensify over time and become more flavourful.

SAFFRON-CANDIED SULTANAS

Makes 150g
(5½oz)

150ml (5fl oz) water
100g (3½oz) caster sugar
Pinch of saffron strands
1 star anise
100g (3½oz) golden
    sultanas

1 In a small saucepan, heat the water and sugar over medium heat. Add the saffron and star anise, and simmer for 4–5 minutes, until slighty thickened. Add the sultanas. Remove the pan from the heat and allow the sultanas to soak for 10–15 minutes to soften and infuse.

PRESERVED LEMONS

Makes enough
to fill a 2l (68fl oz)
Kilner or mason jar

10 unwaxed lemons,
    washed and scrubbed
1kg (2lb 3oz) coarse salt
2 tbsp coriander seeds,
    toasted
1½ tbsp cumin seeds,
    toasted
2 bay leaves, crushed
2 star anise

1 Cut through each lemon lengthways from top to bottom, making a cross, but don't cut all the way through – the lemon should hold together at its base.

2 Mix together the salt, coriander and cumin seeds, bay leaves and star anise in a medium-sized bowl.

3 Gently ease open each lemon and stuff a generous handful of the salt mixture into the flesh of each one, squeezing them together once stuffed and packing them straight into a sterilized Kilner jar, one-by-one. Pack the lemons tightly on top of one another, pressing them down into the jar so that they become covered in their own juices, topping up with the salt mixture around each lemon as you go. Continue with the process until all the lemons have been used, then seal the jar and store in a cool and dry place for 1 month, turning the jar intermittently. The lemon juice will preserve the lemons, softening the rinds in the process. Kept tightly sealed and submerged, these lemons will keep for up to 6 months.

INDEX

UK/US GLOSSARY

aubergine = eggplant
barbecue = grill
beetroot = beet
broad beans = fava beans
butterbeans = lima beans
cannellini beans = white kidney beans
caster sugar = superfine sugar
chickpeas = garbanzo beans
chilli flakes = red pepper flakes
clingfilm = plastic wrap
cornflour = corn starch
coriander = cilantro
courgette = zucchini
French beans = string beans/
  green beans
frying pan = skillet
grill = broiler
hispi cabbage = cone cabbage
natural yoghurt = plain yogurt
onion = scallion
passata = sieved tomatoes
peppers (red/green/yellow) = bell
  peppers
plain flour = all-purpose flour
roasting tray: roasting pan
spring onions = scallions
stock = broth
storecupboard = pantry
sultanas = golden raisins
tea towel = dish towel
tomato purée = tomato paste

10 9 8 7 6 5 4 3 2 1

Printed and bound in China

A Cataloguing in Publication
record for this title is available from
the British Library

An Hachette UK Company
www.hachette.co.uk

First published in Great Britain
in 2022 by Kyle Books, an imprint of
Octopus Publishing Group Limited
Carmelite House
50 Victoria Embankment
London EC4Y 0DZ
www.kylebooks.co.uk

ISBN: 978 0 85783 987 9

Text copyright © Josh Katz 2022

Design and layout copyright
© Octopus Publishing Group Ltd 2022

Photography copyright
© James Murphy 2022

Distributed in the US by Hachette Book
Group, 1290 Avenue of the Americas,
4th and 5th Floors, New York, NY 10104

Distributed in Canada by Canadian
Manda Group, 664 Annette St., Toronto,
Ontario, Canada M6S 2C8

Josh Katz is hereby identified as the
author of this work in accordance with
Section 77 of the Copyright, Designs
and Patents Act 1988

ACKNOWLEDGEMENTS

With thanks to all the devoted and tolerant people I have around me, who have
to mop up the proverbial mess I leave in my wake but enable me to fulfil my
dreams and realise my culinary ambitions in the process.

To anyone and everyone who has ever supported us, be it through your custom
in one of our restaurants, by buying a copy of our first book, or by buying a copy
of this one – thank you.

Louise McKeever, my editor, for continuing to believe in me and the work I put
out, for the tireless work you have put into this book, and for your ongoing
dedication to the world of publishing and cookery writing.

Kyle Books, for believing in this project and enabling it to be brought to fruition.

James Murphy and his entire team (with special mention to Lucia Lowther) for
knowing exactly how to shoot my food and doing it in such a calm and pleasant
manner. Your photography astounds me.

Aya Nishimura, for knowing exactly how to style my food and being so good at
what you do.

The team at Imagist, who reached into my mind and pulled out precisely the
design I was hoping for. You are brilliant at what you do, too.

Eleanor Maidment, for your contribution, and for being a good friend through
the years. Michael Pozerskis (Poz), for your contribution too.

All of my team who work in our restaurants – business partners, managers, floor
staff and those in our kitchen – who help to hold the fort whilst I have my head
down writing recipes, thank you for your ongoing commitment to the cause.

To my mum, Evelyn, & dad, David, whose devotion and generosity knows no
bounds. I am forever grateful for everything you do for me.

Sarah, for tolerating me and my crap. It's not an easy task, I know this.

And my darling Delilah, my gorgeous girl, may you read this book too one day
and be as proud of me as I am of you. x

Publisher: Jo Copestick
Publishing Director: Judith Hannam
Senior Commissioning Editor: Louise McKeever
Design: Imagist
Photography: James Murphy
Food stylist: Aya Nishimura
Prop stylist: Lydia McPherson
Production: Allison Gonsalves

With huge thanks to Gozney (gozney.com) for the use of the Roccbox (page 84)
and to Chefslocker (chefslocker.co.uk) for the Konro Grill (pages 113 and 122).